Faces of Reality
The Story Your Face Is Telling

Jody N Holland

ISBN: 1-63390-051-7
ISBN-13: 978-1-63390-051-6

DEDICATION

I would like to dedicate this book to the people that have helped me learn the science and art of face reading, to those who have allowed me to practice on them, and to you, the person that I am now able to share this information with in this book. I love to simplify the complex. I love to take things that seem daunting and make them easy to understand. My hope is that you take the time to read this, learn the skills of being a master face reader, and apply the lessons in your life. If you do, you will enjoy deeper relationships, greater success, and a stronger sense of confidence in what you bring to this world.

CONTENTS

ACKNOWLEDGMENTS

I would like to acknowledge my family and friends who have pushed me to bring this information to the rest of the world. I am grateful for the push as well as for the support! Thank you to my editor, my graphic designer, my marketing team, and to those who dare to teach something out of the ordinary. I acknowledge and appreciate each of you!

INTRODUCTION

Mastery of any skill takes more than practice. It takes having a depth of understanding that enables you to know what others do not know. It is the understanding of what is known as well as the understanding what is missing that will ultimately create the completed puzzle. In communication, one learns significantly more from what people don't say than they do from what people do say. One is able to learn the inner-most thoughts, feelings, attitudes, beliefs, spirituality or lack thereof, and overall makeup of a person. Great communicators learn who a person actually is rather than simply who they said that they were. One can learn what they are thinking and will know what they are wanting to say, but are holding back. Great communicators learn what another person's model of reality is and what their desire for outcomes is. They engage people in this dance of understanding which unfolds the truth of who they are and creates the interpretation of who you are, or who you want them to believe that you are. Ultimately, it can be looked at as a game. Unless you hold the key to interpret the game, you are simply guessing as to what the next best move will be.

As you begin to understand the truth about people, you will learn that not everything you uncover is good. Some people are self-centered, egotistical, and even violent. You will learn that people who want to be seen as bad are sometimes actually only pretending. They may attempt to project a tough image as a defense mechanism. You will learn what is keeping them from their own truth and how to guide them into understanding themselves as well as the world around them. Nothing in communication is exactly what it appears to be on the surface. It is the substance below the surface, sometimes significantly below the surface, that makes the greatest difference. As you master this art, you will pass through several stages of awareness, each of which will take you closer to fully understanding how to see the world as it actually is.

In the move, The Matrix, Neo was offered the chance to see the truth and nothing more or less than that. I will tell you right now that the truth is not for everyone. The vast majority of people in this world are perfectly content living in a false reality. They are comfortable believing that they are always loved and accepted and that others are not reacting to them negatively. Others are content in believing that they are not liked and that they are the rebel that shakes things up. As you learn how to read the physiological evidence of who a person is, you will learn to decipher the code of good, evil, positive, negative, agreement, and disagreement. You will hone your talent for understanding others. Then, you will move from a good defense into an incredible offense.

You will master the skills associated with leading people in the direction you wish for them to go mentally. You will learn the art and skill of pulling people in a specific direction, based on how they see themselves. From a coaching perspective, this is one of the most incredible skills that you can develop. By knowing people instantly, you can lead them and persuade them much easier than others could. As one of my mentors has admonished me multiple times... "Always use your powers for good and not for evil." For that reason, you will learn the intent of the art. As your instructor, I can only present you with what things should be. Ultimately, how you use them will be up to you. My hope is that you use this information to make the world a better place. For me, I have used it to garner a deeper understanding of humanity. I have used it to create authenticity in my relationships. I have used it help others move their lives forward.

BECOMING A COMMUNICATION GURU

On this journey, you will begin where each of us does. You will be unconsciously unskilled. You will be unaware of what is missing. You have made it to this point in life and possibly done alright. You might have some success in your career, maybe even a lot of success. Your family loves and respects you, hopefully. But even if that isn't true and even if every part of your life is currently NOT what you had hoped for it to be, the application of this information can help you to get the ideal version of reality that you want. It is in picking up this information that you begin to look for what is missing. There is something that other people know that you don't. Those people that have what you want, that have seen the top of the mountain and felt the rush of the wind in their faces as they achieved greatness, those were the seekers who once picked up a book and said, "what else can I learn?" By taking the first step on this journey, you are prepared for the tough part.

As the journey begins, you become consciously unskilled at the things that matter the most. You gain an awareness of what is missing in your life, but don't necessarily have the skillsets in your grasp. This is a tough place to be, but it is also liberating. It is liberating to finally realize there is more out there. It is freeing to know there are skills you can learn that will launch your life, your career, and your mission to the next level. Over the years, I have met lots of people who do not wish to accept new information. Instead, they cling to the new information they were taught as kids and shun new ways of growing or connecting. Some people fear change more than they embrace possibility.

This is decision time for you. Do you accept there are things you need, that you don't have, that will change the world in your mind, and make things different? Will you accept that you can and will learn new realities for communicating? If you can embrace the need to learn, the lack that exists, and the truth that you can learn, then you will move to the next step in the journey.

You will become consciously skilled at the art of the communication guru. You will see the world that is unseen to most people. You will unlock a new reality of connecting, communicating, reading people, and gaining a deeper understanding of humanity, but you will have to focus. This is not a time for you to simply rely on a single sense. You must apply skills with deliberate thought and intentional practice. It is in the focused application of new information that you will gain your skills. This is no easy task, though. Faces of Reality is not something that you read one time and simply master. It isn't a single session or training that engrains this into your psyche. Mastery of face reading is the deliberate, focused, and skilled application of the information in this book. That level of focus is what makes the learning stick. Are you willing? Are you ready? Will you make the effort to be at the next level? I hope so. If you are willing, I am ready to help!

The final stage of your learning will take you to a level where you are unconsciously skilled. This stage is where you achieve the first level of mastery! Most people never reach this level because of the time and focus required of them. Some simply learn a few things and make the minimal effort required to get by. These people have never experienced the joy and exhilaration of mastery. They have never known what it was like to simply know something without having to strain to recall it. When we know something completely, we are able to integrate the skill into who we are. This mastery is what makes all the difference.

When I started in martial arts, my instructor would have me throw the same kick over and over and over again. I have no doubt that I threw a front snap kick so many times that I could execute that kick without any thought about how to hold my hips, legs, or toes. They would simply go where they were supposed to go because it had become a part of my cellular memory. This level of mastery is required of us to become truly authentic at communicating. Achieving authenticity is the only way to find where you are truly meant to be.

BECOMING AUTHENTIC

Becoming authentic takes concentrated effort. You must commit to mastery in order to become authentic. In Bruce Lee's book, <u>The Tao of Jeet Kune Do</u>, he talks about becoming "like water" as you learn. As you learn something completely, you take on the shape of the skill in the same way that water takes the shape of any container. Authenticity arises from action and adaptation toward mastery. Mastery arises from focused learning. Focused learning arises out of a desire for mastery. So, authenticity is born of desire, cultivated by effort, and revealed in action. As you discovered in learning the four stages of mastery, reading a single book or taking a single class is only the beginning. You are on a journey toward becoming a grander version of yourself.

Welcome To Your Journey!

1 FOREHEAD

The study of the face will begin from the top. The forehead reveals the manner in which a person makes decisions. Decision-making has been studied for hundreds of years. Is this person emotional? Are they logical? How do they respond in tough situations? How does their concept of self, who they see themselves to be, impact their interpretation of the world around them? These are all questions that help us understand the people that we interact with. The characteristics of the forehead, its lines, its shape, its slope, help us to understand how the person processes inputs.

The human brain operates much like a computer processor. Once the code is in place, the processes kick in every time there is a stimulus. It is as if we are kick starting a code-driven, predictable, and fairly consistent response pattern. The challenge is that it is not just the inputs in a person's life that creates the code by which they operate. The simple reality is that the inputs are one thing, but the label of the input is everything. When a person experiences something in life, they give meaning to the experience. It is the meaning that matters in programming how the mind works, not just the experience.

Think about someone you are close to who seems to make decisions opposite of the way that you do. You see the same world around you, but you seem to label it very differently. Our context for decision-making changes the reality that appears before us. Someone who is very logical will tend to strip away the emotional context of a situation. Likewise, someone who is emotional will seem to be incapable of accounting for the logical components of the decision that they are making. Emotional people reverse engineer logic in order to support their decisions, and logical people try to color in the blank spots with emotion after they have used logic to make their choices. We do what we do because it fits with the manner in which we are most comfortable interpreting the world around us. The world is not the same for everyone. In fact, the world reflects our minds. Our minds do not reflect the world. They construct it!

Structures of Decision Making

Another way of looking at decision-making would be to see that we operate primarily in either cognitive or emotive structures. Cognitive decision-making means that we are tapping into the portion of the brain that houses language and logic. This portion of the brain is responsible for your cognitive response patterns when making decisions. Some would refer to this as the new-brain or the evolved brain. This is not to say that logical decision-making is better than emotive decision-making. It is just a newer portion of the brain. The limbic center of the brain houses our emotions and is sometimes referred to as the croc-brain or the primitive brain. This would be the portion of the brain that houses your emotions and is responsible for your feeling interpretation of events. It is important to understand which portion of the brain rules the day in making decisions because it will modify the strategy and mode of connecting with another person. To connect or persuade or inspire another person, you will need to know what will work with them. To lead another person, you will need to master connecting like they would connect.

Most have heard the saying that you cannot put a square peg into a round hole. From a communication standpoint, this is incredibly true. You cannot use emotional appeals on a logical person or logical appeals on an emotional person. Your communication needs to be a perfect fit for the person you are with at that moment. This is akin to having the master key of connection with that person. The correct communication style unlocks the possibilities and builds an image of a perfect fit between you and that person. This is critical because their label of the interaction is what makes it work or not work.

When looking at a side profile of a person, you will see that the forehead is either rounded or it is flat. Think about the section of the forehead that exists between the outside edges of the eyebrows. When you look at that section of the forehead, you are trying to identify the shape of the forehead. Below are a two pictures that are labeled as flat or rounded. In the following sections of this chapter, you will also be exposed to the various aspects of how a person makes decisions based on either a flat (logical) or rounded (emotional) forehead. You will learn which people tend to overthink things and which people tend to go with their street smarts in the situations that they face. You will learn who is tenacious and whose mind tends to jump from one thing to another (shiny object syndrome ☺). You will also learn how the labels that exist in a person's mind have impacted and will always impact the world that comes into focus for them. This first chapter outlines how a person thinks, why a person thinks the way that they do, and how to connect with them based on their thinking style and patterns. A variety of forehead components play into the interpretation of decision-making. You will want to look at the height, shape, lines, and other characteristics on that person's forehead. Each of these reveals one more clue as to how their mind works.

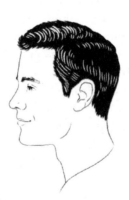

The above picture depicts a flat forehead. Individuals with a flat forehead prefer to use logic as their primary decision-making tool. The use of logic comes more naturally for them. They can use emotion, but it takes more focus and more energy.

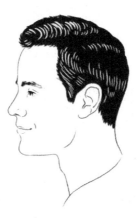

The above picture depicts a rounded forehead. Individuals with a rounded forehead tend to prefer emotion as their primary mode of decision-making. This is what comes more natural for them. They can use logic, but it takes more focus and energy.

Self-Concept

Reciprocal self-determinism is one of Albert Bandura's cognitive theories stating that a person's behavior is influenced by and influences both their environment and their thoughts. (Bandura, 1986) We interpret our environment in a certain way and, therefore, behave according to those expectations. When we interact with the world around us, our view of actions, influenced by our view, results in an interpretation of the world which is colored by our original view of the world. For example, I see myself as a successful writer. I therefore believe that the world wishes to read what I have to write. I therefore write and seek out validation of the belief that I have of myself. You see yourself in a certain light and then seek out ways to act according to that belief and then to validate the belief based on those actions. This means that we will see the world as emotional and will require emotional contexts if we are emotional decision-makers and as logical and needing logic if we are logical decision-makers. So, let's dive into the other aspects of the forehead and what they mean to us as we interact.

Keep in mind that you are who you are and where you are because of the labels you have given to the experiences of your life. What you believe about you will ultimately determine what you think, how you act, and the results that you attain in life.

Emotional Decision-Making

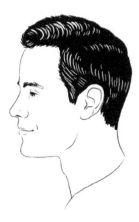

Individuals who make their decisions rooted in emotions will respond more positively to emotional appeals, connect at an emotional level with others, and use their emotions to make sense of the world around them. Each of us is searching for a way to explain our experiences. The emotional thinker will reach into their mind and search for how they feel in relation to the situation. They often react more quickly to situations as well as more intensely. When they fall in love, they fall hard. When they get angry, they get more intensely angry. When they are persuaded, it is because they "feel" that the other person is taking them in the right direction. One of the common mistakes that we make is to try to persuade an emotional decision-maker with logical appeals. It simply doesn't work! They get particularly frustrated with people who tell them things like, "You need to calm down." They don't want to be logical because it is not natural to them.

You will want to pay attention to the full shape of the forehead. There are people who will have a mostly rounded forehead with a flat spot in the center. If this is the case, you will know that they begin with emotions and then try to bring logic into the equation as they are thinking through things.

Logical Decision-Making

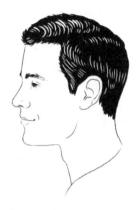

Logical decision-makers want to know the sequence of events and the steps that have landed us in this place (whatever the situation may be). They prefer to look at the facts and measure the potential outcomes of various scenarios. They focus their energy on making sense of a situation in context of logic and predictability. They become particularly frustrated when they are dealing with individuals that are overly emotional and can't seem to "get control of themselves" in order to have a logical conversation.

Again, pay attention to the entire shape of the forehead. If the forehead, in the side view, is rounded on the outside edges with a little flat portion in the middle, the person will likely start with their emotions and end with logic.

Apperception of Reality

Our perception of the world around us relates to us making sense of an experience that we are going through at that moment. The challenge is that we never make sense of the world in a void. As we experience the world, we reference back to the previous experiences we have had and to the meaning we have given to each of those experiences. The meaning, or the labels, that we placed on experiences that were similar to our current experience will have a significant impact on the manner in which we evaluate the current experience. Think of it like a filter in your brain. Everything you experience has to sift through the filter of your past experiences and the meaning those experiences hold for you. When it is sifted, it is changed. The meaning an experience has is unique to each person because their labels and experiences from the past are unique to them. Therefore, each new experience is simply a filtered variation of a previous experience. As people make decisions, they are making them through the lens or filter of what they have experienced previously in life. They are not making decisions based solely on their current emotions or logic. Many of those filters are revealed in the face. Does a person filter twice, or overthink things? Does a person filter quickly, or use the instinct? Knowing how a person filters is important to knowing the person.

Structures Of The Forehead

A forehead can be tall, average, or short. The height of the forehead should be judged in relationship to the overall size of the person's head. It is not a specific measure, but rather a proportional measure. Someone with a tall forehead will tend to think deeply about things that they are experiencing in life. They will then overthink those things. They have an intense need to evaluate the possibilities and often irritate even themselves in the process. They second-guess the possibilities and try to play out every possible scenario to the point of exhausting themselves and those around them.

Tall foreheads also tend to use intellect in their processing. They prefer to think through things, search for experts in that particular arena, and rely on the input of multiple other people in order to make a decision. This search for validation relates back to the use of intellect in processing the world and making decisions.

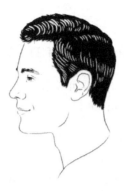

Short foreheads, proportional to the rest of the head, tend to use their instincts to make decisions. They tend to play out scenarios related to how others will react to them and what the likely outcomes will be, but seldom seek out validation for the decision. When a person has a shorter forehead, they can often be seen as using their "street smarts" instead of their book smarts. This isn't better or worse than a tall forehead. It is simply different.

Short foreheads don't spend as much time second-guessing themselves and their choices. They make a choice, move forward, and evaluate as they go. They have a tendency to simply learn from their mistakes and move on, rather than dwelling on what happened, who was at fault, etc. They experience frustration the same as tall forehead individuals do, but they do so because of getting knocked down and having to learn a lesson rather than because they were analyzing all of the possibilities before they acted. Short forehead individuals tend to act much more quickly than tall forehead individuals.

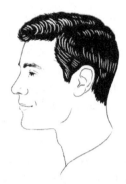

Lines On The Forehead

The lines on the forehead reveal the neuro-patterns of a person's thoughts. Like any other aspect of the face, the lines can change as the person's view of the world and habits within the world change. We are what we believe about ourselves. When the belief changes, the face changes with it.

When there are lines that run all the way across the forehead without breaking, this would indicate that the person stays attached to a thought and a direction from beginning to end. They will have a tendency to finish whatever they start. You will notice distinctive lines running all the way across from roughly the outside edges of the eyebrows without a line break when the person's thoughts do not wander.

On the other hand, when a person has multiple lines that are disconnected, you will notice they tend to jump from idea to idea quickly. The more squiggly and broken lines on the forehead, the more the person's mind tends to jump around. These folks are often very creative, but are better at starting than they are at finishing projects.

When the lines are broken at the top of the forehead and go across at the bottom of the forehead, they start very strong and will have a tendency to lose interest toward the end of a project. When the lines are broken at the bottom of the forehead and go across at the top of the forehead, they tend to jump around with lots of ideas that never get started, but they tend to finish strong on the ideas that actually do catch on.

When a person has three lines that run across their forehead all of the way without a line break, these folks have a tendency to focus all the way through a project. Historically, this is the mindset that yields the highest ROI (Return On Investment), and this type of person ends up with the most success in life. Success can be defined in terms of money, completion of a mission, or any other facet that fits the person.

Recap of the lines

Notice that the line is continuous across the forehead. This indicates that the person both tries to and prefers to finish what they start. The solid line indicates a tenacity in their thoughts that makes it difficult for them to let go of things until they are completed. This would be the person that feels they have to get their house in order before going on vacation. They don't like to leave things undone or half done. Their mind relaxes much better when their tasks are complete. When they cannot complete their tasks, their mind tends to keep reminding them that they are not quite done yet.

When the person has lines that break across the forehead, their thoughts and focus tend to break as well. Notice how the picture demonstrates a line that begins and then has a space and then picks up again. A person's mind tends to jump around more when they have broken lines. Some would call these folks "distracted," while others would call them multi-taskers. The simple reality is that they do not have the same compulsion to finish that the straight-line folks have. They prefer to have several things going at once and are more frustrated if they have only one thing to do instead of three or four things to do. They require more stimulation to stay engaged.

You will notice, when you look at people as they wrinkle their foreheads, whether the lines are all the way across the forehead or are broken across the forehead. You will also notice that a person with a line that breaks more than once across the forehead will need more variety than a person whose line breaks only once. Botox is not our friend in face reading because the lines are a great way to understand focus.

Imagination Lines

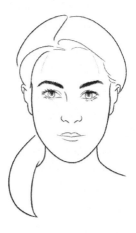

Imagination lines look like a muscle that begins about three quarters of the way out on the eyebrow and goes up and out toward the top outside edge of the forehead, where the hairline would begin. If you place your right thumb and index finger approximately one inch apart and then place your right thumb on the outside edge of your right eyebrow, this would be the starting point for the imagination line. Trace your thumb and index finger up and out at roughly a 65 degree angle toward the outside edge of the forehead. This is the path of the imagination line.

You will notice that it appears that the muscle can flex, particularly as the person furrows their brow and/or clenches their jaw. The imagination muscles represent a person who is more inclined to imagine new ideas, new solutions, new concepts that have not been presented before. They tend to be better at putting together various aspects of information in a new and interesting way. They see a world that could exist as if it does, and they do so before it ever has.

Think about someone that you know that has a great imagination, can visualize positive end results before they have even begun working toward the result, and who seems to have a vast creative capacity. This person likely has these muscles sloping up and out from the eyebrows to the top of the forehead. If one side is more defined than the other, that would indicate that they have a greater capacity in one side of their life than the other.

Slope Of The Forehead

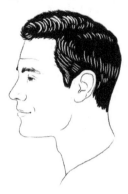

The slope of the forehead tells a bit about their mental interaction with those around them. When the forehead appears to slope forward, the person is more mentally aggressive. This is particularly true of people who are emotionally based decision-makers. If the forehead slopes back, the person tends to be better at being reactive. They are often known to be quick-witted. The slope of the forehead measures the mental application of thought.

When you put the various components of the forehead together, you begin to see how the person processes information and thinks through problems. If you find that someone has a proportionally tall forehead, that is rounded, and that seems to bulge forward, this is a person who is mentally aggressive using their emotions and who tends to overthink things. As a general rule, you would need to be very relaxed and accepting to get along with this person. A person who has a rounded forehead, regular height, and whose forehead slopes back would likely be a person who uses wit and charm to connect and who is pretty relaxed much of the time.

The key to understanding the thoughts of a person is to understand how they process. This gives you a basis for how they are likely to label the events in their life. This understanding of how they will label is what will prepare you to engage with them more quickly and to connect more deeply.

2 EYES AND EYEBROWS

It has been said that the eyes are the windows to the soul. This could be taken a step further and said that the eyes are the projection of the soul. The manner in which we construct the world inside of our brain is based on the roughly one million photoreceptors in the eye working in harmony to take the external world and reconstruct it inside our internal world.

Visual Cortex

The visual cortex takes data in from the outside world and then allows the brain to translate what the outside world looks like as well as what it means. Inside the brain of a human is an apperception mass. This is the portion of the brain that holds the labels or meanings of past experiences. When we witness something new, we first look back into our memory banks for something that would be similar to what we are currently experiencing. Once we find something that is similar, we overlay the old experience or object on top of the new one. This act of apperceiving the world is one where we give meaning to that which we experience. This means we are taking in data, but it is not pure in its translation. Every experience we have that stimulates feeling or emotion will also stimulate a meaning or label. When you see someone who looks like another person whom you love or care for, you will see more of the beauty in that person. When you see someone who looks like a person whom you cannot stand, you will see more of the negative characteristics. The visual cortex works in concert with our past experiences as well as with our emotional centers in order to see what the brain wishes for it to see. This means that we are seeing a distorted image of reality at all times. We are seeing what our brain wishes for us to see instead of what our eyes are bringing in without filter. This is important to remember because you will interpret a person more than you will see them. What you see in the person's face depends on what you are looking for. The more you practice seeing the characteristics of a person's face, the more those features will appear in your visual processing, or primary visual cortex.

Reflective – Medium – Deep

When you look at a person's eyes, you will notice a strong reflection, a mild reflection, or a depth to them. At times, their eyes will not look deep, but rather they will look hollow. It takes practice to notice the manner in which light reflects from the eye, but once you have mastered this, you can tell the emotional maturity of the person. The practice is in focusing on the bounce of the light or the absorption of the light into the person's eye. When a person's eyes seem hollow, it is as if they are disconnected from the reality of their world which translates to a far off look in their eye. I have often referred to the eye reflection as a measure of the depth of a person's soul, but it could be seen as maturity as well.

Reflective Eyes

Eyes that reflect most of the light that is hitting them will represent a less developed maturity in the person or a soul with less depth. This would mean that they will tend to be more reactive in the nature of dealing with the world around them. Think about an adult that allows their emotions to cause them to have fits when they don't get their way. Think about how they react to people instead of thinking through what is happening and choosing a response. When the light reflects strongly off the person's eyes, they demonstrate a younger soul. These people tend to focus more on finding fun and less on long-term pursuits. They prefer to enjoy the here and now and will be more likely to avoid difficult or long pursuits. For them to think long-term would require more energy than the other types of eyes. Remember, reflective eyes are a mirror to the manner in which the person takes in information. Strong reflection means that less is coming in from the consideration of that which is outside of them.

Medium Reflection In The Eyes

Medium depth to the eye, or some reflection but not a lot, would indicate that the person has the capacity for perspectives from outside of them as well as inside of them. This person will, at times, react to situations instead of responding. They will generally feel what they want on the inside and will then process whether to consider the people around them or simply themselves. Individuals with a medium depth of light into the eye will generally be better at thinking about medium range goals. They want to have fun, but not at the expense of being able to pay the rent this month.

Low or No Reflection – Appearance of Depth

Depth in the eyes indicates a more mature, or older, soul. An old soul is one who connects well with people older than they are, who generally likes to learn about the past and think about the long-term future. They generally see difficult or different people as a way for them to learn and grow themselves. They don't shy away from challenging relationships because they are fascinated by the idea of why a person is doing what they are doing. You will often find people with depth to the eyes in relationships with a very eclectic group of people. They have more of a tendency to want others to simply be who they are and less of a tendency to want others to conform to them. The depth also represents a maturity in perception. They are able to see from the other person's perspective and adapt according to what is needed in that situation.

Deep Set Eyes – Eyes That Bulge

Deep Set Eyes (Left) and
Eyes That Bulge (Right)

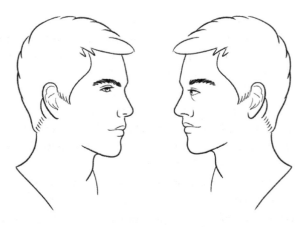

The physical location of the eye related to the eye-socket and face tells us about the person as well. Eyes that sit back in the eye socket and do not come close to crossing the imaginary line down from the brow ridge to the cheek bone represent a person who is more likely to take things in than to send things out. This type of person tends to wait and see what others are saying and how others are feeling before contributing their thoughts. This is important to note because one who observes often gets more information than one who projects.

Eyes that sit out from the eye socket, particularly those that cross that imaginary line from the brow ridge to the cheek bone, will be more likely to share what they are thinking. Often times, this person will say things in a manner that would draw attention to them. They tend to seek out attention as well as becoming very frustrated when they are interrupted. They will see others as particularly rude if they speak over them when they are sharing something. If you do have a friend whose eyes bulge out a bit, it is most likely they will become agitated if people are not paying full attention to their stories. If you wish to test the theory, try interrupting their sentence two or three times and observe their emotional reaction to this.

Eye Lashes – The Long And The Short Of It

Longer Eyelashes (Left)
Shorter Eyelashes (Right)

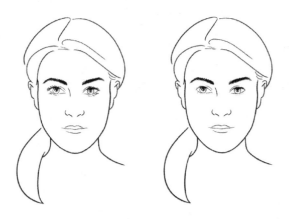

While it is true that many people modify the length of the lash, the length still tells us a story. People who need a break at the end of the day will have naturally longer lashes. Those who condition themselves to need a break at the end of the day will tend to extend their lashes artificially. As a people, we are influenced by the behaviors that we see in others. When a person gets to the point of wanting to be left alone for 20 to 30 minutes at the end of their day, they will either grow longer lashes or attach them artificially. Those who are less inclined to hide away for a bit at the end of a day will have naturally shorter lashes. They will also feel ridiculous wearing extended lashes if their friends talk them into the extensions. This need for time to unwind is important to note. If you are in a relationship with a long-lash person, give them space at the end of the day. The easiest way to know the true length of the eyelashes is to look at the lower eyelashes. Very few people ever extend those. They are generally only extending the upper lash.

Brow Ridge

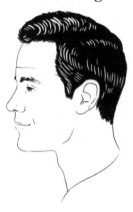

Some people will have what appears to be a ridge that runs horizontal across the eyebrow portion of their face. If you place your index finger, as if pointing, across your eyebrows and then raise and lower it, you are checking to see if there is a bump that moves your hand out. This bump, or ridge, indicates whether or not the person has rules and systems that they need in order to function. The stronger the brow ridge, the more the person requires their own set of rules and systems in order to be successful. A strong brow ridge means a strong need for rules and systems. You will see that people who operate with lots of rules often have very strong ridges developed. Think about some of the career law enforcement and career military people whom you know. Those that excel in these structured environments tend to have that need for structure. Interesting, however, some people with a brow ridge will simply make up the rules of their game and then live by those rules. The ridge doesn't mean that the person follows all rules. It means that they will have rules and systems that they follow, even if they don't make sense to the people around them.

Flat – Rounded – Arched

There are three basic eyebrow structures that can be observed. Just like the eye lashes, eyebrows can be shaped, and they often are. The eyebrow shape will tell you the best way to approach the person based on how they are likely to initiate and engage with others. When a person shapes their eyebrows, they are attempting to get others to engage with them in a specific manner. In the next section on the thickness of the eyebrow, you will learn how a person attempts to change the perception of the mental strength when they thicken the eyebrow. For now, let's look at the three shapes that tell us how to approach the person.

Flat Eyebrows

Flat eyebrows indicate a person who approaches others with task before relationship. They tend to focus on what needs to be done and how to get it done before they focus on connecting with others. You have interactions with folks like this who will ask about the job or task and then say, "and how are you?" This is not meant to be offensive by the other person. They just tend to have their mind clouded with the task until it is satisfied. Once it is satisfied, they are able to become relational.

Rounded Eyebrows

Rounded eyebrows indicate a person who approaches others with relationship before task. This person will need more time to build rapport and will value the connection with the person before they are able to fully focus on the tasks to be completed. They need to know that they can connect with a person before they can fully engage on the tasks to be completed. Once they feel a connection, their mind is able to relax, and they will be more confident in knowing that they can do work with, complete tasks with, and engage in getting things done with them. Their need for relationship must be satisfied in order for them to be fully focused on the task at hand.

Arched Eyebrows

The third eyebrow shape is that of an arch that typically sits about two-thirds of the way out on the eyebrow. The arch indicates a need for keeping things in control. An arch on the left-hand side or their left eyebrow indicates a need for control in their personal life. An arch on the right-hand side or their right eyebrow indicates a need for control in their working/school life. When a person has an arch on both sides, they simply need control. Control can be misinterpreted though. Control is not really about controlling others around them. Instead, it is about a need to feel "in control" in situations. This person's stress level rises significantly when they feel that things are out of their control or cannot be managed effectively. When approaching this person, keep in mind that they have a strong need to be right. Give them the chance to come up with solutions and to be right about the process that they follow.

It is very possible for a person to have one shape on

their left eyebrow and another on their right eyebrow. People will often have different views on the way to approach things in their personal life versus their professional life. A person may be relational at home and more task oriented at work or relational at work and more task oriented at home. They may need control in one side of their life and have no need for control in the other side of their life. Pay attention to the subtle differences, and you begin to truly learn the story that the person's face is revealing to you.

Thick or Thin Eyebrows

Thin Eyebrows

The amount of eyebrow reveals the manner in which and the direction in which a person tends to experience the emotions of others. Someone with thin eyebrows has a tendency to absorb and experience the emotions of the people around them. If someone around a thin eyebrow person begins to cry, it will likely trigger the need to cry with that person. Thin eyebrows indicate an absorption and experience of other people's emotions. This perception of the emotions of others goes beyond just absorbing feelings though. It serves the person well in reading what is going on with a person beneath the surface. It is like an emotional sonar built into the brain of the person. They are sending out signals that check the depth and type of emotion that is being experienced. This sonar pings back to the person and says, "this person you are around is sad or happy or angry or…" and lets the individual adapt to the emotional needs of that person. It is not a sign of weakness to cry when another person cries. It is a sign of strong empathy to be able to feel what another person is feeling.

Thick Eyebrows

Thick eyebrows indicate more of a projection of emotions, rather than an absorption of emotions. When a person has thick eyebrows, they project their emotions out instead of taking emotions in. This does not necessarily translate to the person being mean. They could be a great motivator because they project positive emotions to those around them. They could project any emotion they are experiencing or have chosen to project. They tend to be less effective at properly interpreting the emotions of others, however. They focus more on what they wish to project into the world, and they put it out there.

You will often see people draw, or even tattoo, thicker eyebrows on than they really have. This is an attempt to appear more mentally tough than they really are. They will often do and say things that do not represent how they really see themselves. This attempt to project mental strength is often not well received. People tend to pick up on inauthenticity. Someone trying to appear mentally stronger than they really are may lash out at others, act out against rules, or simply try not to engage much with others in an attempt to not come across as weak. You will also see people get rid of their eyebrows completely and then draw them back on. When a person cannot reshape their thinking, they tend to reshape what they see when they look in the mirror. Dr. Maxwell Maltz, psychiatrist and plastic surgeon, said that even when a person reshapes their outer body, nothing changes until they reshape their inner image of themselves. Step back from the mirror and look within. What do you see when you look at you from the inside out? This is the image to focus on because it is the mind's projection of self. Change this projection, and one's entire world changes.

Eyebrows Tucked Beneath The Brow Ridge

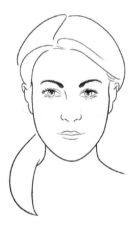

The eyebrows will sit above, on, or will extend below the brow ridge. Where the eyebrow sits is important to note. For example, if the person's left eyebrow sits higher than their right eyebrow, they have higher standards in their personal life than they do in their business or school life. When a person's right eyebrow sits higher, their standards are higher at work or in school. This variation in where the eyebrow sits gives you a heads up as to which area is more critical to the person.

When the eyebrow tucks under the brow ridge, or extends below and just under the brow ridge, this indicates that the person has a smaller filter between their brain and their mouth. In other words, they are more likely to say what they are thinking without regard for filtering their thoughts. This often results in these folks wishing they could take things back. Once it is said, it is said. Some will filter on one side of their life and not the other. Most people who lack the filter, however, tend to lack the filter in both sides of their life.

Fade In – Fade Out
Outside Fade (Left)
Inside Fade (Right)

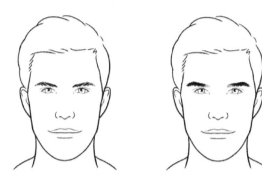

Eyebrows can be faded on the inside, faded on the outside, even, or possibly even connected. When an eyebrow appears to be faded on the inside left eyebrow, but not the right one, this indicates that the person experienced mental struggle in the early part of their personal life. When it fades on the inside on the right eyebrow, it indicates the experience of more struggle in the early part of their work or school life. The right side is a bit more difficult because it could relate to school and not work or to work and not school. When the eyebrow appears to fade out on the outside of the eyebrow, it indicates more struggle in the second part, or more recent part of their life. Left is personal and right is professional. When the eyebrow appears to grow across and come close or actually connect, this indicates an overly active mind. Someone with the eyebrow that grows across will have more trouble sleeping because it is very difficult to shut their mind off. They are continuously thinking and often can't turn it off. One proven method effective in relaxing the mind of these folks is that of progressive relaxation or self-hypnosis. There are a number of guided self-hypnosis apps that can be downloaded. They tend to work very well to give the person something else to focus on, rather than the monkey-mind that is running amuck.

One Eye is Bigger

When one eye appears to be larger than the other eye, this indicates a stronger focus on figuring out that side of the person's life. For example, when the right eye appears to be larger than the left eye, the person is trying harder to figure out their career than their personal life. This doesn't mean that they don't care about their personal life, however. This simply means that they are expending more effort to figure out their professional life. It could mean that their personal life is clicking along great and does not require figuring out. The same is true in the opposite direction. When the left eye is larger, the person is more focused on figuring out their personal life than their work life. When you know the person's focus area, you can help facilitate their success in the area that requires more help.

Keep in mind, most of the differentiation we are

discussing here will be subtle. Most of these differences require you to pay very close attention to notice them. The more you focus on the differences, the easier they become to notice. As a reminder, do not go around telling people what is going on with them unless you are invited to do so. Most people don't like to be told who they are and what is going on with them. As a general rule, I pay attention to everything a person's face is telling me, but I reserve the negative for my own knowledge and share the positive. This keeps you in people's good graces as well as giving you the advantage of fully knowing what is going on with a person.

3 NOSE AND CHEEKBONES

Taking In The World Around Us And Projecting Who We Are

Whether thinking of taking in the world from our eyes, our ears, our touch, or our nose, we are always processing meaning through our experiences. Gustatory interpretation (a fancy way of saying interpreting the world through our sense of taste) and Olfactory interpretation (a fancy way of saying interpreting the world through our sense of smell) both have a lasting impact on us as well.

Think back to a happy time at your childhood home or the home of your grandparents. Think about a smell indicating that the world was right. I have a clear smell still in my mind of what homemade buttermilk biscuits smell like when they are baking in the oven. My grandmother would get up very early, around 4:30 AM, and begin to make biscuits from scratch almost every day. As the biscuits would rise in the oven and begin to turn a light golden brown, the scent would drift into every room in their farmhouse. I associated the smell of the biscuits with being in a safe place, knowing that I would be well fed and ready to take on the day. Even now as I write this, I can smell the biscuits in my mind. When I do, it takes me back to that time of simplicity and peace and comfort. I can literally taste those buttermilk biscuits as I imagine the smell of them. The positive emotions from that time come flooding into my mind as I remember the smell and taste.

Each of us likely has a time that was a great smell, whether food, or a certain experience, or something of the like that brings back positive emotions. The use of smell has a tremendous impact on our emotional state. Candle companies, scent manufacturers, incense and perfume manufacturers understand that the human psyche is influenced greatly by this sense. Consider what your emotions tell you when you smell certain smells. Also, consider how those smells seem to come back to you as you simply remember them, even though are not experiencing them in the moment. Your mind can and often does manufacture scents. Your mind interprets the world around you, but it also interprets the world within you. Your nose tells a story in partnership with your mind!

The story being told is one of emotional connection. The various aspects of our emotional experience can be drawn back into our awareness when the scent is present. When we are asked to think of a scent, it stimulates our emotional centers in our brain and begins to bring back those memories. The interesting part of this is that our brain can be triggered by a word or a smell or the sight of something or someone. Try, as an experiment, to introduce the smell of something that was a good memory to someone that you know and see what their reaction is to the smell. You will typically find that they are more calm, more engaged, and experience more happiness in the presence of the good smell.

The Bridge of The Nose (Thickness and Bumps)

Thick Nose Bridge

Thin Nose Bridge

The bridge of the nose tells the story of a person's will as well as times when their will was tested beyond its limits. When you look at a person's nose, you notice the thickness of the bridge of the nose (width). This thickness demonstrates the thickness, or toughness, of their will. A wide nose bridge that runs the length of the nose indicates a will that is unyielding and strong from start to finish. A thinner nose would indicate one who would have to have outside influence in order to maintain their willpower. They will need a team of people who will help to push them in order to ensure that they accomplish what they have set out to accomplish.

Bump on Nose Bridge

When a person has a bump on their nose, this indicates a time in their life that their will/spirit was broken to the point that they felt they needed to protect themselves. Anytime we are pushed beyond what our will would allow, it leaves an emotional scar. In this case, the bump on the nose indicates that scar, and it is manifested in the form of defensiveness in that person's personality. What is fascinating is the bump represents a specific time in the person's life when they became defensive. By itself, it will not tell us what the defensiveness is, only that they have defensiveness in their personality.

As the human mind develops from birth to around 7 years old, the brain waves slowly shift Delta waves (slower frequency) into more consistent conscious process, or Beta range (higher frequency). There are other wave patterns in between these, but the important thing to remember is that we shift from awareness and outside influence toward internal conscious control. Until around the age of 7, we do not have enough conscious processing to become truly defensive from our experiences. This is why the nose registers defensiveness beginning at the age of 7 and throughout the rest of a person's life. Often times, the person will not know exactly why they have defensiveness in their personality. If they think back through their experiences in their life, however, they will come to a time that has had a lasting negative impact on them. The story from this time in their life created the impact. When a person is made to feel helpless in a situation, they tend to bury the emotions of the experience. It could have been a time in the person's life, or it could have been a specific interaction with a person. The higher up the bridge of the nose (toward the forehead), the younger the person was when they became defensive. The lower down the nose the bump is, the more recently the person became defensive.

The tricky part to perceiving their defensiveness at the correct age is in guessing how old the person is when you are reading their face. Within a half inch of the end of the nose would register as within the last 3 or 4 years of the person's life (very recent). As you are reading their nose, simply ask them if something happened around the age of "x" that has had a lasting negative impact on them. My word of caution here is that this can surface strong negative emotions in the person if/when you ask them about that time. One other technique I have used that has proven to be effective, is to simply tell them that I am sorry for whatever happened around "x" years-old or in "x" grade. I then tell them that I think they are a great person, regardless of what that person did to them or what happened back then. Most people respond well to reassurance and comforting words.

The Sides of The Nostrils

The sides of the nostrils (outside) tell the story of self-direction versus team direction. The caution on reading the nostrils is that there are a couple of ethnicities which tend to have this feature, regardless of their thoughts, so proceed with caution. People who have a strong line in the outside edge of their nostrils have a tendency to be more independent in their thoughts and actions than those that do not have a line. Some people will have a line on one side and the other nostril will be smooth. For example, if the person has a line on the right and not on the left, this would indicate that they are more independent at work and more cooperative at home. To clarify, independent does not mean uncooperative. It means that their first mode of processing is to look within instead of outside of themselves. I have found this part of the story should also be talked about with caution. Independence and defensiveness can both trigger a reaction in the person. Therefore, some of this information is for you to know and use to your advantage in connecting with the person, rather than sharing everything that you know.

The Septum

The septum is the center bottom of the person's nose, or the part that sits in between the two outside edges of the nostrils. The septum tells us the person's drive toward both mission and the answer to the question... "Why?". When a person has a septum that comes down lower than the outside edges of the nostrils and it does not appear that the outside edges are pulled up or curled back, this would indicate a strong drive towards mission and understanding why things are the way that they are. The way that you know if the outside edges look pulled up or curled back is that if you are looking at the person and they are looking straight forward, you would be able to see into the person's nose. We are looking for the nose that you cannot see into, but the septum looks like it comes down from the nose. People with this feature tend to do very well in jobs where they are given the opportunity to make a strong difference. Non-profit work, mission work, and work that helps other people directly will help to fulfill the needs of a person with a lower septum. You will also find that this person has a stronger tendency to ask the question, "why." They want to understand the reasoning behind things. They tend to seek out purpose in the things that they do.

Point: Someone that does not have a lower septum is simply driven by something other than mission or understanding why. They are not a bad person or less compassionate. They simply have a different drive.

The Variation in Nostril Size

When you look at a person, you will often notice variations from one side of the face to the other. One of those variations is the size of the nostrils. Remember that the person's left side of their face relates to their personal life and the ride side of their face relates to their professional life. Professional includes school for those who have not yet graduated from formal education. When you notice that the right nostril is larger than the left and the left appears to suck in a bit, this indicates that the person has insecurities related to their personal life. If you notice that the left nostril is larger than the right and the right appears to suck in a bit, this indicates that the person has insecurities related to their professional life. If both nostrils appear to suck in from the outside to the inside, this indicates insecurities in both sides of their life.

On the other hand, when the nostrils tend to be full (not flared out, but full), this indicates a lack of insecurities and a stronger self-confidence. The nostrils will look proportional to the face. They will not appear small or large, just proportional.

When the nostrils appear to be overly large as compared to the person's face or what would seem to be normal, this often indicates that the person is overly confident in self. This typically results in the person putting themselves in a position of taking on more than they can actually handle. They tend to overload themselves. This often results in them becoming frustrated, as well as the people that thought they could count on them.

Caution: This read is typically just for you. Like the defensiveness in the personality, very few people will be okay with you saying they are insecure or overconfident. Knowing where the person stands in their self-perception is really important, but sharing it with them is not so important. Use good judgement in what you share versus what you simply know.

The Tip of The Nose (circle and line)

When you look at the end of the nose on a person, you will notice that some people have what appears to be a circle, or ball, on the end of their nose. This is very common for people who are reporters for any media outlet. This feature indicates a desire to be in the loop, or in the know. People with this feature don't like being left out of the inner circle of knowledge. In order to communicate effectively with this person, let them know that you wanted to make sure they were in the loop and share information beyond the minimum. You want to make sure they feel included.

Bridge of the Nose is Concave (seems to dip inward at the top and out toward the tip, like the inside of a circle)

When the bridge of the nose is concave, this indicates that the person has a strong capacity for repetitive tasks. This would be great to know when asking a person to do something that might seem mundane or overly repetitive to another person. When someone has the capacity for repetition, this trait is fantastic for any work or job that is predictable each day. For example, someone that works in a production line and does the same task and motion all day long would do better if they had the concave nose bridge. This simply indicates that their mind is wired for this kind of work. It is not a reflection of IQ or capacity for thought, but rather an indication that they would be better than others when it comes to repetition.

High Cheekbones

Cheekbones are more predictive on females than they are on males. The human brain is wired differently from male to female. Keep in mind that the number of connections between the two hemispheres (this is the section known as the corpus colosseum) of the brain is significantly greater for females than for males. This means that logic and emotion are interwoven in females. This also means that emotional events have a tendency to be more impactful on females than on males (general rule but not true in every single instance).

High cheekbones can indicate one of two things. They either indicate that the person was in the middle of a lot of drama when they were in Dr. Morris Massey's third stage of psychological development (14-22 for females and 14-26 for males), or indicates that the person has a love/passion for travel. Interestingly enough, when the person is in drama during the socialization period of development, they often long for a way to physically escape the situation through leaving the situation. They desire to travel out of the situation. So, either way, a person tends to desire to travel when they have high cheekbones. They desire to leave the bad situations behind, or they desire to discover new lands, or new to them.

Angular Features versus Soft Features

Angular Features (Left)
Soft Features (Right)

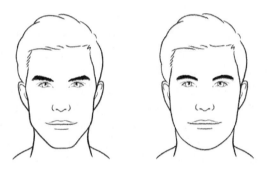

When a person's face is more angular, they have a tendency to be more sharp or harsh in their response patterns. They tend to react more quickly to things they are faced with and will often be more harsh in that reaction.

When a person has softer features such as a rounded face versus an angular face (cheeks, eyes sockets, jaw, and chin), they tend to be more warm and accepting, less judgmental, and more inviting. This is one of the reasons that people with soft features are often better at relationship selling. They have more of a natural tendency to be warm and inviting because they tend to have the outlook of desiring a softer and warmer relationship with others.

At a root subconscious level, we tend to judge people upon their appearance. Many of us have trained ourselves to have a secondary thought that is less judgmental, but many people have an initial thought about the people they encounter. It is our biopsychological tendency to determine whether a person is friendly or dangerous when we first meet them. Our natural reaction is to judge those with sharp or harsh features as more of a threat and those with softer features as less of a threat to us.

In this chapter, I have discussed a lot about defensiveness and reactions to events that we have faced in our lives. This judgement of our experiences is a reflection of the stories playing in our heads. For example, if someone were mean to you when you were younger, you would have made up a story in your own mind that would explain the situation. The story you made up would have become a part of the story of you. This means that you would begin to judge other aspects of your life based upon this story. You would have begun to filter your current perceptions through the lens of the story.

When I was in 2nd Grade in Canadian, TX, I had a teacher who became frustrated with me for not speaking up enough in class. I was brand new in the school and was hanging back to see what everyone was like. Back then, in the 70's, teachers would diagnose what was wrong with a kid without necessarily testing them for anything. That is a huge no-no now by the way. This teacher indicated that I needed to be in special math, or math for kids that weren't very good at math. She also put me in special English. The teacher for special math proceeded to tell me that I was stupid in front of the other kids in the class. She did this multiple times to me over that year. I remember the story that I told myself at the time. My story was that I wasn't dumb, she was just a crappy teacher who was incapable of teaching a lesson. I also told myself that the other teacher was incompetent and was looking for ways to not have to have as many students in her class. For years (over 30 years), anytime a person indicated that I was not capable of something, or that I might have done something dumb, or if they used the word stupid, I would react aggressively. I didn't fully understand why I got so angry until I traced back to this time in my life and examined the stories I had told myself.

At some level, I had wondered if they were right, so I pushed myself incredibly hard to be seen as intelligent. Upon going back to that time in my mind, I decided that I needed a story that made me less defensive and served me better in life. After all, I had created a number of arguments with my wife as well as people in business when they indicated I might not be the smartest guy in the room. I wrote a new story. My new story was that the two teachers knew I pushed myself hard when I was questioned, and they knew that I would be a world-changer if I had the right prompting and the right motivation. They simply didn't know the best way to do that, so they put me down. That was their purest form of how they could inspire me to become the full expression of myself. In my mind, I went back to that time, and I thanked them for pushing me to become who I am today. As I write this book, this is my 17th book to publish. I have done business in over a dozen countries and all across the United States. I have almost two dozen CEOs that come to me for advice on a regular basis. I am thankful for who I have become, and I am not sure that I would be here if they had not ticked me off so much. If either of those teachers ever read this book, I want to tell you thank you for hurting me because I found my strength through that.

Your story is your story. You can rewrite it anytime you desire. You can change the meaning of the story or the intent of the person who plays a main role in your story. It is not up to them. It is up to you. The past has already happened, but the meaning of the past has always been and remains... up to you. Ask yourself the following three questions if you are attempting to rewrite the meaning of your past.

1. What would I have to believe in order to be happy?
2. If I wanted to believe that, could I?
3. Do I want to?

When you ask yourself those three questions, it

leaves no room to remain in a defensive and hurt state without accepting the fact that you have chosen that state. Choose the state of mind which best serves your success moving forward. By doing so, you take control of your mind and your life. You intentionally and consciously create meaning in your life. You also no longer allow people from your past to maintain control over your present. You become the master of your fate and the captain of your soul. There isn't any reason to allow others control over your emotions. You are in charge of you, and you have always been capable of experiencing the life you desire. I would encourage you to meditate on the meaning that you wish to have in your life. I would encourage you to visualize those negative experiences from your past and rewrite the stories into ones that suit you. If you know that you have a choice, which you do, then it stands to reason that choosing happiness only makes sense.

4 MOUTH AND JAW

With each aspect of our senses, we are meant to both take things in as well as share things out with the world. Many of us would believe that the mouth is designed primarily for sharing. After all, I remember hearing from adults over and over again as a child... You have two ears and one mouth, use them in that proportion. The adults in my life wanted me to listen and learn more than sharing my opinions. The mouth is very interesting though. Our Gustatory senses (fancy way of saying our sense of taste) is connected with our emotions. If you remember from the last chapter when I talked about the smell of my grandmother's biscuits in the morning, every time I have that recollection, my senses work together to stimulate both a memory and an emotion. When we taste something that was from our childhood, we often have the flood of feelings from that time in our lives. The mouth is an incredibly powerful tool. We can speak life into others. We can speak hate into others. We can speak peace or violence. We evoke emotions in ourselves and in others with the words that we say.

From a listening standpoint, others hear the words we say. This provides content for the message. They also watch and listen to the manner in which we speak those words, which gives them context. We are able to deliver the same message as someone else and have it interpreted completely differently than the other person did. Simply by changing your tone, cadence, and pitch, you can completely change a message. Add to that the fact that we are constantly interpreting others based on their body language and facial expressions, it is no surprise that our words are such a small part of how we are interpreted. 93% of what is interpreted from our message is based on tone of voice (which includes pitch, cadence, and tonality) and body language (which includes facial expression and the rest of the movement and positioning of the body). Only 7% of our message consists of the words themselves! This is not to say that the words are not important. They are. In fact, without the words, the other 93% of the interpretation could not and would not happen.

The crazy part to the world we live in is we are constantly backfilling the tone of voice and body language into the messages that we receive through technology. When you receive a text, an IM, an email, or any other electronic message, you look at the writing of the message, recall what you know about the person, and infer the 93% that might not have been there. The mouth plays an integral part to our communication. It gives life to our thoughts, momentum to our desires, and either builds up or tears down the people around us. I remember making the conscious choice that I wanted to use my verbalization of thoughts in a more positive way. I wanted to leave people feeling better about themselves and this world instead of feeling worse. This meant that I had to make a choice with each and every interaction to choose my words carefully. I had to be in charge of my mouth instead of letting it be in charge of me. When you make that choice, you set yourself up for success. You set yourself up to build others up and to bring life, joy, and success to their experience of you.

At a biological level, we are constantly evaluating others. We are looking at the shape of the features of their face and making a call as to what those features mean. The intentional interpretation of the features allows us to be in control of those "automatic thoughts" and to determine how we wish to proceed with them. Our amygdala controls our fight or flight response mechanism. Our pre-fontal cortex controls our language and conscious processing. When we decide to use our language on purpose, we begin to reshape the interpretations that the limbic center (emotions and gut reactions) of the brain would have otherwise made.

There are features on a person's face that you like. Often times, you don't know why you like them, you just know that you do. The reasoning behind your like or dislike of facial features relates to your experience with people who have those features. At a subconscious level, you have been cataloging every experience you have had with others and giving labels or meaning to those experiences. With every new experience, you add to the label, peel it off and change it, or simply reinforce it. The mouth and jaw are the components of the face that project who we are into the world. They tell the story of us as a contributor or participant in the world. You feel a certain way about a strong jaw or narrow pursed lips, or any other feature observed. You begin to build a profile of what the person would be like to interact with and how they would treat you. This is all done somewhat automatically. The beauty of understanding this aspect of a person is that you are able to consciously evaluate a person rather than simply reacting through subconscious suggestion. Let's dive into what the various parts of the mouth and jaw mean.

Mouth Width (wide versus narrow/small)

Wide Mouth

A person whose mouth is wide in proportion to the size of their face will tend to be more gregarious and outgoing. They are more likely to share what they are thinking and more likely to have something to say. To be gregarious is to be a bit louder, a bit more likely to share thoughts, and a bit more likely to draw attention to themselves. Tony Robbins has an incredible and wide smile on his face. He has something to share, and he goes out of his way to share with the world around him. Tom Cruise also has a proportionally wide mouth. Although their messages are quite different from one another, they tend to share their messages with those around them. Think about the people in your life. Do you know someone who has a proportionally wide mouth? What are they like in conversation? What are they like in a group of people? What are they like at a party? Most likely, they are somewhat loud, share their opinions, and tend to not hold back when it comes to drawing attention to themselves.

Small Mouth

The smaller mouth, proportionally to the face, indicates a person who is more business-like. This doesn't mean they are not fun to be around. It does, however, mean they tend to want to accomplish their work before they play. They tend to struggle a little more with humor or coming across as fun-loving. They are excellent at keeping things on track, though. They are the kind of person you would want around if you needed to accomplish something of value. They will likely become very agitated if you question their intent when it comes to the work that they do. They take their work seriously and want others to know that they are focused on success.

Crooked Smile

Keep in mind that the left side of a person's face relates to their personal life, and the right side relates to their professional life. If they are still in school, then school is considered their professional life. When a person has a smile that goes up and to the left, they will have a tendency to use sarcasm and wit in their personal life. They do this more often to deflect tension or to ensure that they are liked, accepted, etc. When a person has a smile that goes up and to the right of their face, they tend to use sarcasm and wit in their professional life in order to deflect tension, gain support, or build comradery. This type of charm typically serves the sales representative or business development specialist well.

One Lip Larger

When the upper lip is larger than the lower lip, these people are more prone to agitate others and create drama in their relationships. The larger upper lip indicates a person who has trouble understanding that others would disagree with them or question them.

When the lower lip is larger than the upper lip, these people tend to seek out validation and reassurance. The pouty look is just that. They are needing others to tell them that they are okay and to reassure them for who they are. This is assuming that the upper lip is not overly tight. When it appears that the upper lip is tightened, or pressed in toward the mouth, it is a different meaning. The lower lip being more plump and full with the upper lip appearing natural or proportional to the face is the look that demonstrates the extra need for attention and validation.

Tight Upper Lip

Chances are you were told as a young person, at some point, to keep a stiff upper lip. This was usually told to young people when they were about to start crying or if they had just started crying. In order to stifle the emotions they were feeling, they would pull their upper lip in, take a deep breath, and repress their emotional state. When a person has a tight upper lip, one that appears to be pulled or flattened toward the face, they have a tendency to repress their emotions. They are not as likely to express what they are thinking or feeling. Often times, this person will help others deal with their emotions without dealing with their own emotions. This is not necessarily a good thing. When we do not experience our emotions, they stay trapped inside of us. I am not suggesting that people let loose on others with their emotions. Instead, I am suggesting that people find a healthy way to process their feelings. This type of person often becomes very frustrated with having to help others when they are in need of help themselves, but do not know how to ask.

Show Upper Gum Lines When Smiling

When a person smiles and their upper gum line shows, they tend to be a very strong giver. The more the upper gum line shows, the more of a giver they tend to be in relationships. The downside of being a giver is they tend to attract takers into their life. They tend to get into relationships with people who are needy or mean or self-centered. Although they do not always end up in bad relationships, it is often the initial frustration they deal with. Ideally, this type of person learns that they should seek out another giver in order to keep the relationship more balanced. Whether with a friend, a coworker, or in a romantic relationship, this feature reveals that they seem to try hard to make sure the other person is happy. At some point, they will likely become frustrated that their needs are not being met. They often feel they are being taken advantage of, used, or simply not being appropriately valued.

They ask themselves questions like, "Why am I the one who is always giving in this relationship?" and then wonder why they keep pouring themselves out for others. My caution is for them to stay focused on finding someone who values their relationship, whether friendly or romantic.

Crooked Lower Teeth

People whose lower teeth are crooked tend to set impossibly high standards for themselves. They tend to beat themselves up when they make a mistake and often look for what they did wrong before what they did right. This tendency toward self-criticism is a part of the manner in which they process. Even if they get their teeth straightened, they will tend to crowd back up unless the person learns to love themselves for who they are and to see the good in themselves.

Gap Between Upper Front Two Teeth

The gap between the upper two front teeth can indicate one of two things. Often these two things go together. The gap indicates a lack of either emotional or physical presence of a father in their lives when they were young, or it indicates a strong drive towards goals and accomplishments. From a psychological perspective, we are often seeking to prove that we are worth loving. Men grow up seeking the approval of their father for their accomplishments. Women grow up seeking the approval of their father as a figure that demonstrates right relationships. I realize this is one of the more controversial features on a person's face. Most of us don't want others to think that we need their approval. Many of us don't want others to think we did not have the physical or emotional support we needed from our dad. Some get upset that this feature is tied to the father and not so much to the mother. The caveat to this is when the mother steps in and fills the role of the father, it can often fill the gap in needed approval during the formative years. Regardless of how we look at it, the gap indicates either something is missing from their emotional or physical presence needs from their childhood, or it indicates a need to demonstrate success through goals and accomplishments.

Jaw Lines
Wide Jaw Line (Left)
Narrow Jaw Line (Right)

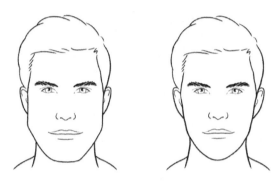

The jaw line demonstrates both determination and the direction of that determination. Think about someone with a particularly wide jaw. The portion of the jaw that matters is the outside edge, below the ears, and back from the chin.

The wider jaw structure indicates a strong determination to accomplish. They have a tendency to latch on to something and not let go until they have succeeded in accomplishing their goal. I would refer to this as the English Bulldog Tenacity. They get a grip on accomplishment of something particular and then keep going and going and going. They wear people down with the persistence.

The more narrow jaw line indicates a person who is more likely to defer to the others around them. They tend to like cooperation and want to simply move things forward. They are less focused on having their own way and more focused on ensuring that they achieve group consensus.

Like other aspects of the face, sharp or angular features in the jaw will demonstrate a more sharp expression of self. More angular features often reveal a person who is ready to assertively, possibly aggressively, react to a situation. On the other side of that, the person with a more rounded jaw line tends to draw others in and set them at ease. They are seen as more cooperative and easier to trust. The rounded features typically do well in customer service and relationship selling. The sharper features tend to do well in situations where a show of force might be necessary.

Ripples in the jaw line

When you see what looks like three ripple lines in the jaw of a person, this indicates a stronger aggressiveness. This can come across as intense determination or it can come across as dangerous aggressiveness. The ripples in combination with a wider jaw denote a person that will aggressively pursue their goals and will likely run over anyone that gets in their way. Be a bit more careful about pushing the person with the ripples in their jaw line.

How we project ourselves emotionally and actively into the world is seen in the mouth and jaw line. Pay close attention to the manner in which a person projects themselves and look at the features of their face. When you are able to learn how to adapt yourself in order to accommodate the person you are with, you are best equipped to keep the relationship positive, inspire specific projected actions from that person, and move things forward. This can apply to negotiation, building a friendship, starting a romantic relationship, etc.

5 CHIN

Deterministic Approaches To Self-Image

There are a variety of theories that describe the manner in which we become the people that we are. For example, Albert Bandura indicated that we are often the result of environmental determinism. This is a model of becoming who we are based on the factors that we are exposed to in our environments. Bandura theorized that children who are raised by violent parents would in turn become violent parents because that was the conditioning that shaped them. This idea of environmental determinism essentially tells us that our childhood is the reason why we are who we are as adults. (Bandura A. R., 1961) Bandura does account for variations in mental illness that would modify the manner in which a person interprets their formative experiences.

I would argue that a large number of people see themselves through the lens of being the product of their raising. They believe the circumstances that surrounded them as they became adults, and that continue to surround them as adults, is impacting their judgement. I think there is some real merit to this theory. After all, people tend to see themselves in a certain light and as an average of the people whom they spend time with. Think about your own life. How many of your experiences do you believe have shaped your thoughts and actions?

Others believe we are simply the result of genetic determinism. One's intelligence, behaviors, personality, and ultimately their actions could simply be attributed to the genetic markers that exist for them. This would mean that regardless of how we wished to view ourselves, our primary characteristics would not change. I have a lot of trouble with this one. My main issue with the idea that we are not able to change is the sheer number of observations I have made of people transforming from one view of themselves to a completely new view of themselves. This new view then resulted in a brand new set of behaviors for that person.

Whether you look at the theories of Skinner, Bandura, or any of the other determinists, the overarching perspective is that you have very little choice in who you become. You were born to be a certain person. The environment around you in combination with your genetic makeup creates a reinforcement map that guides you to where you were always going to go. The situations you are exposed to then get interpreted to mean what they need to mean in order to preserve your belief system. This preservation of beliefs ensures that you continue to see yourself as you should.

Humanistic Approach To Self-Image

The humanistic approach to development goes in the opposite direction. This approach rests on the principle of free will. Each person has the ability to determine, at any point they choose, to direct their life in any way they desire. This approach is more in line with societal views on responsibility, crime, punishment, and success. The humanistic approach makes a lot of sense to the person who reads faces. After all, a person's face will make subtle and consistent changes based on changes in one's beliefs. My theory is that what we believe creates who we are. People will judge themselves, or evaluate themselves, based on one of three primary angles. They will either create change or avoid it based on one of two viewpoints. The viewpoints will determine the ultimate direction of the person's life. The self-evaluation will determine the lens in which the person views the experience of life.

The Viewpoints

We either have an internal control point or an external control point. The determinist will operate with the idea of an external control point. This means that a person is never fully responsible for their actions. The circumstances in which they find themselves along with their genetic makeup will determine what happens in their life. They believe that the current characteristics of who they are will forever remain the characteristics of who they are. They are not capable of change because it isn't possible in their mind. They are a product of their circumstances. When things go wrong, those things were outside of their control. They could not have done anything differently. Someone with an internal control point would operate with the viewpoint that they are in control of their choices. Regardless of the circumstances in which they find themselves, they always have a choice about what they should do next. They believe that they can choose their actions, their emotions, and even their attitudes. They operate with the knowledge that they are never helpless.

The Lens of Perspective

The first perspective that a person could have is that they should judge themselves based on relationships. This would mean they evaluate their life based on how their relationships are as well as what others might think of them. Having a concern for what others think is neither the right way nor the wrong way to self-evaluate. It is one way to self-evaluate. This perspective looks more at the impact of actions on others than it does impact on self or goals.

The second perspective is that of self-evaluation based on goals and accomplishments. This type of person looks at life through the lens of what they are able to get done. They take more pride in accomplishing their goals than they do in developing deep relationships. This is not to say that they are not relational or that the relational folks don't accomplish goals. They simply see a different perspective on what it means to be successful. Goal driven individuals are less likely to be great listeners, however. They have a tendency to dislike listening to people who make excuses and can often be a bit harsh in their response when others don't share the same drive as them.

The third perspective is that of self-evaluation based solely on an internal self. This is the person who is not driven by the goals and accomplishments that might be seen as critical to others, nor are they driven by depth in relationships. Instead, they have an internal image of who they are and tend to maintain that image regardless of what is going on in the world around them. This self-perspective can be seen as self-centered within most Western cultures. This type of person is often labeled as "self-centered." They are simply less tuned in to the goal drives of others or the relationship drives of others.

Square Chin

To have a square chin is to adopt the perspective of being driven by goals and accomplishments. This person is often treated more like a leader at a young age and will tend to develop those qualities because of the reinforcement of others. Many images of great leadership have a strong, square chin. Captain America is a great example of someone who is on a quest to accomplish greatness and who has an incredible square chin.

Round Chin

To have a round chin is to adopt the perspective of being driven by relationships. This relational drive is reinforced through youth when this person tends to listen more to those in need. You will find that people who are driven to help others, to counsel, or to simply be the friend whom others turn to, will have a nice rounded chin. They tend to develop depth in their relationships as well as to have more friends than the goal-driven individuals.

Pointy Chin

When the face in somewhat angular and the chin appears to come to a point, this is the perspective of self-evaluation. This self-perspective often gets reinforced when this person cares less about the goals that others place before them and then cares less about the others around them. The struggle with the person who focuses on self is that Western culture is not set up for this although it operates as an individualist culture. Young people are often taught to share and collaborate by their parents. If a child is taught to care about themselves first, then they have a tendency to be less effective at sharing, collaborating, caring, etc. They reinforce themselves as more important and increase the perception of self-centeredness.

Different From One Side of the Chin To The Other

It is possible for one side of the chin to appear rounded while the other side of the chin appears more square. If this does happen, it simply means that the person evaluates themselves differently in one side of their life versus the other side of their life. If the chin appears more square on the person's right side and more rounded on the person's left side, they are more driven by goals at work and more driven by relationships at home. Remember that the right side of the face has to do with the external world (work) and the left side of the face has to do with the internal world (personal).

Chin Dimple

To have a dimple in the chin, or what looks like a dot-shaped indention, is to have a stronger passion. The dimple indicates that the person will experience stronger emotions in the things that they pursue. This could relate to personal relationships as well as work ventures. They tend to approach things with an intensity that others might view as overly strong or might simply admire.

Separated Chin or Vertical Line Down The Center of The Chin

I don't like to use the term "butt-chin," but it does bring a certain visualization to the forefront of a person's mind. The up and down line in the middle of the chin represents a person who tends to draw attention to themselves in order to deflect tension with others. This type of person will make themselves the "butt" of the joke so that others can laugh at them. They often cut up and bring a levity to group situations. This is a fantastic characteristic as it indicates that they care for others and want them to have positive relations with one another.

Pulling It All Together

The perspective we have as we go through life is critically important. Knowing the manner in which a person evaluates themselves will help you know which types of compliments, appeals, and influence tactics are right for that person. If a person primarily cares about goals and accomplishments, then talking to them about what others might think of them is NOT going to be very effective. Focus on who they are and adapt your approach in order to connect at the deepest possible level.

6 EARS

VAK Learning Model

The concept of understanding a person's modality of learning has been around for over a century. The idea of breaking this concept of learning styles into a few simple areas has been refined and refined and refined over the years. Educators of all types, whether corporate educators, public school educators, or even Montessori style educators, all want to know how a mind absorbs information in the best manner. Jean Piaget, best known for his study of the cognitive development of children, was fascinated with how young minds developed as they acquired knowledge, as well as the very nature of intelligence. He devoted much of his life to his Theory of Cognitive Development, outlining the four stages that a child passes through as they develop. My favorite quote of his discusses how we have the capacity and the right to learn on our own, and that educators often rob a child of the right to truly develop by their manner of transferring knowledge.

"When you teach a child something, you take away forever his chance of discovering it for himself."
--Jean Piaget

Learning is not simply the transfer of information from one being to another. Although education often seems like a transfer of information, true learning is much more. Many times, education is about taking what is in the book and transferring it from the book to the teacher to the student and back to the test without really understanding it. That is NOT learning. Learning is the process of taking outside inputs, internalizing them, creating a framework of understanding, and then applying the information within the context of the real world. I am primarily an auditory learner. I learn best by hearing what is said and then talking through the information. I am also a very logical person. I asked repeatedly when I would be using the information taught in school. Most of the time, my teachers would simply respond that I would be using it on the upcoming test. That was a disheartening answer to me, as it is to many others as well. Earning a credit is one of the least inspiring things I have done with my time. However, learning something that I can use to help others... THAT is worthwhile.

As you consider the learning model that applies to you, ask yourself a few key questions.

Scenario: You are getting instructions on how to go to a new friend's house for a visit. Is it better for you to...

A. See a map of the route and have your

friend trace out the route for you?

B. Have your friend describe detailed instructions on the steps that you will follow and have the chance to ask questions?

C. Drive there one time with your friend either leading you or riding in the car with you to give you instructions?

A – Visual
B – Auditory
C – Kinesthetic

Visual Processor

The visual processor needs to see a map, a chart, a graphic, or at least construct an image in their head. When a problem arises, the visual processor will create a mental image of the moving parts, and will often see things move around. They have a tendency to say things like...

- I can see your point.
- My view is...
- I would imagine that...
- My picture of what would work best is...

They use words that describe seeing or visualizing something. Their focus is on getting the right mental roadmap in order to make sense of whatever is going on in the conversation. Reading is generally a good way to remember things for this person, as well as having things demonstrated for them.

Auditory Processor

The auditory processor needs to talk through things. They need to hear the other person, as well as hear themselves in order for the thoughts to fully make sense. Auditory processors tend to like logic, sequence, and thinking through things. They will say things like...

- My thought on the subject is...
- I would like to talk more about...
- The steps that make the most sense to me are...
- Can we have a dialogue about this before we...
- Let's talk through all of the steps...

They use words that describe thinking, talking, listening, logic, and sequence. They respond better to commercials where they hear a message rather than if they read it or watch it. Auditory processors may struggle with reading unless they reading quietly out loud. This process helps them to retain the information more effectively.

Kinesthetic Processor

The kinesthetic processor needs to experience things, feel things, and do things. When they are in motion, their brains are more engaged and better able to process. It is ideal for this person to be in motion when they need to talk through something. If you sit them down, tell them to stop fidgeting, don't allow them to doodle, and ask them to talk through what is going on, you will be very disappointed in the outcome. Kinesthetic people are often good at activities that allow the process of thought and action to merge together. In school, if they were allowed to doodle during a lesson, they would remember more of the content. Many teachers are either auditory or visual. They either want students to read the text and then be tested over it, or they want students to listen to the lecture and be tested over it. Kinesthetic learners need to experience the application of the information in order to internalize it. They might say things like...

- This doesn't feel right.
- I don't know how to explain it but, my gut says...
- Let's stop talking and do something.

They do not speak as much or as eloquently as the auditory person, and they do not write or visualize like the visual person. They learn through action and emotion. They need experiences.

Too often, we forget that people are a blend of these three styles of learning. Each of us has a primary style, but we also have a secondary style. In order to get your message across to a diversified group of learners, it is important to vary up the wording and the practice of sharing information. The most effective manner of getting people to see, feel, and understand the message is to...

- ☐ Describe what you wish for the person to know and give a chance for Q & A.
- ☐ Demonstrate what you wish for the person to know.
- ☐ Have them demonstrate the skill while you coach them.

By doing this, you are covering auditory, then visual,

then kinesthetic learning models.

Neil Fleming of New Zealand (Fleming, n.d.) was the first to systematically define the VARK learning model. The "R" in his model stands for Reading/Writing. It is a blend of the visual and auditory styles. Fleming indicated that there are those who learn best through reading on their own and writing out their thoughts. For those that excel in online schooling, this is the style that likely describes you.

Olfactory and Gustatory Processing

Our sense of smell and our sense of taste have a tremendous impact on the emotional state that we are in. When I was taking a class on non-verbal communication, one of the project teams had us fill out a brain-games test on the 3rd week of class and again on the 12th week of class. They did the same experiment with 4 different classes within the communications department (different groups of people). The results that came back were fascinating. Consistently, the groups that filled out the brain teasers when there was a floral scent on the corner of the paper were all happy to participate. The classes that filled out the brain teasers when there was a putrid scent on the paper were all unhappy to participate. What is interesting about this is that the scent was so faint that it was not consciously perceptible. Nobody was consciously aware there was even a scent on the paper! Wow! This means even the faintest of scents will have a direct impact on the attitude we have when performing tasks.

Scent and taste trigger our emotional response patterns. It is really important to remember we are continuously impacted by the setup of a room, the smell of a building, the taste of our food, etc. Be intentional about creating the right atmosphere within your home as well as within your business, so people have the right emotional setup to experience interacting with you.

Small Ears and Large Iris

A person who has small ears (compared to the size of their head) and large irises will be a visual processor. They will take in more through their sense of sight than through their intuition/emotion, touch, or through hearing. This type of person will respond well to visual presentation of materials. If you are trying to influence them, they will need to see your point, not just hear it.

Large Ears and Small Iris

A person who has larger ears (compared to the size of their head) and small irises will be an auditory processor. They will take in more through the auditory process than through intuition/emotion, touch, or visual representation. This type of person responds well to hearing your point of view. They need time to create a predictable model for information. Be articulate in your presentation of materials with them.

Folded Back Ears

When it appears the outside edge of the ear is folded back to the point where the inner ear ridge sticks out further than the outer ear ridge, this is a kinesthetic processor. This means action, emotion, intuition, and touch are the drivers for the manner in which this person processes. In order to influence them, you will need to activate the emotional response centers of their brain. Don't try to explain everything. Instead, talk about action and how they will feel when everything goes just right.

Correlation To How We Interpret Being Loved and Appreciated

Gary Chapman wrote the book, <u>The Five Love Languages,</u> to explain the manner in which we feel loved. He also describes clearly the likely manner in which we will show love to others. Chapman's book helps people to understand the way we process the world in relationships. You can find it at: www.5lovelanguages.com. I would encourage you to pick up a copy, as well as to take his test. In the book, he describes each of the following love languages.

- Words of Affirmation – This would likely be for the auditory processor.
- Acts of Service – This would likely be for the kinesthetic and the visual processors. For the visual processor, it would need to be an act of service that could be seen or have a visible result.
- Receiving Gifts – This would likely be for the visual processor.
- Quality Time – This would likely be for the kinesthetic processor if it is quiet time where you are simply together. It would likely be for the auditory processor if it is time visiting.
- Physical Touch – This would likely be for the kinesthetic processor.

Knowing the manner in which a person feels loved is important. It gives you an advantage in connecting with others more quickly. Even if you are not attempting romantic love, each of us wants to feel valued. Your quick reference guide is below…

- Visual
  - o Gifts or visible acts of service
- Auditory
  - o Words of affirmation or quality

time
- Kinesthetic
    o Physical touch, acts of service, or quality time
    o Acts of service are particularly relevant for demonstrating love for the kinesthetic processor.

Inner Ear Ridge

The inner ear ridge is a representation of one's ability for self-reflection as well as an indicator of whether a person can accept that they might be wrong. When a person does not have an inner ear ridge, or it is flat inside of the ear until the outer ear ridge is reached, this indicates they have a very low likelihood of believing they could be wrong. Often times, you will see no inner ear ridge on one side but not on the other. A person might believe that they could be wrong at home but not at work, or vice versa.

Notches On The Ear

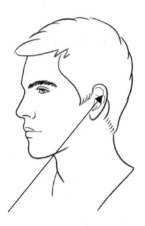

Similar to rings in a tree trunk representing different seasons, humans develop notches on their outer ear ridge to show significant seasons of their life. At the very top of the ear, this would represent 18 years old. You can work your way forward on the small section of the outer ear ridge and go down to 14 years old. You can work your way back on the outer ear ridge and go all the way to the ear lobe's edge, which would represent roughly 40 years old. With a notch or a bulge in the outer ear ridge, there is an indication that a person has experienced a significant shift in their perceptions. On the left-hand side, this represents their personal shifts in perception. On the right-hand side, this represents their professional/external shifts in perception. We don't necessarily know what the shift was for this person just by looking at their ears. We only know that they experienced a shift. When a person shifts their perception, they have begun to see, feel, or process experiences differently. Often times, you can tell when a person got married or divorced by where the notches or bulges fall on the left ear. I will normally ask the person what happened when they were "X" years old. They will usually say… "I got married then," "I met my significant other," "That is when I got a divorce," or they recall a significant emotional experience from that time. It is really amazing to be able to peer into a person's life and know when things changed for them.

Ear Lobes (size and horizontal lines)

Horizontal Lines In Ear Lobes

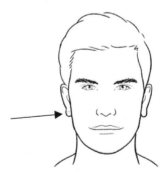

The ear lobes indicate heart health. When a person

has a horizontal line that looks like a fold on an ear lobe, this means they have blood pressure issues. If it is on the left side, the stress and pressure relates more to their personal life. If it is on the right side, it relates more to their professional life. Sometimes, it will be on both sides. This means that both sides of their life have them experiencing more stress than they realize.

Large Ear Lobes

Larger earlobes indicate a stronger need for a spiritual connection in their life. Look at the size of the lobe compared to the size of the ear. Everything is relative to the other parts of the person's face. A person with larger lobes may not need what we would normally define as traditional religion, but they will need a spiritual connection in order to feel whole, complete, and happy. Smaller ear lobes don't mean that a person doesn't like spirituality or religion. They simply mean that the person doesn't need as much spirituality in order to feel content in life.

The ears are an amazing indicator of how our minds are processing the world around us. When we look, listen, and feel, we are doing so based on the way the world rolls around in our heads. Not everyone will process the world just like you. When considering the love language or the processing or the interpretation of reality that a person experiences, keep in mind that we each have a primary style. Also keep in mind that most people have a secondary style which impacts their interpretation as well.

7 HAIRLINE

The hairline of a person indicates the manner in which they approach work as well as whether or not their mother (or the female that was dominant during their formative years) was a strong influence on their worldview. This is a fascinating topic because we are continuously wondering why people are who they are and why they approach work the way that they do. Imagine being in a job interview and already knowing which person has a greater capacity for working long hours. Imagine knowing who needs a relaxed atmosphere in order to function better. Knowing some of these basic things will position you to ask better and more strategic questions. It will position you to lead people, influence people, and inspire right action more effectively.

Let's go back to what life was like during your formative years. Dr. Morris Massey indicated that there were three stages each of us passed through as we developed our perception of the world around us.

In the first stage known as imprinting, we developed our core personality. We learned how to see ourselves, how to determine right from wrong, and how to go from simply being in the world to understanding that the actions we take impact the world around us. In the second stage known as modeling, we learn how our labels of the world begin to shape our experience of the world. During this second stage, how we work and what work means to us will be largely determined. The age of 10, according to Massey, is one of the most critical years of our lives for the development of values. We find people whom we look up to and whom we wish to model. If your early heroes are hardworking, driven, and focused on getting the job done, this can and will impact the way that you see work.

Consider the hairlines of some of the people that you admire the most. Male or female, knowing the shape of the hairline over the forehead can give you some great insights into the working lives of the person. You can begin to understand if they believe that being relatable is what makes work better, or if they thing long hours and dedication are what make work better. You can discover if their world was tumultuous when they were young, or if things ran more smoothly for them. You can discover if they believe that work should be a bit more formal or a bit more casual in order to be effective. As you study the hairlines of others, you are studying their worldview on work.

Rounded Hairline

Just like in other features of the face, when a person has smooth, rounded features, they are more on the relational side of life. They are more likely to listen to others, look for ways to relate, and seek out work that allows them to be connected with others. They will look for ways to generate meaning in their lives related to connecting with others. The rounded hairline is the relational hairline. Think about some of the more relational people that you know at work. They likely have this roundedness to their hairline.

It is also very likely that they had heroes when they were young who focused on helping others or building others up. Their heroes could have been family, teachers, coaches, or even comic book superheroes. As we mature through the stages of development, we latch on to people who embody what we believe to be right and just. We strive to become like them and to demonstrate the qualities and characteristics that they exhibit.

Square Hairline

When a person has a squared off hairline, they are more likely to be focused on the task side of life. For example, someone with a square hairline would have a stronger capacity for working long hours. This is because they are driven by the completion of the task. Being driven in this manner, their self-concept is connected directly to their productive output. They will, therefore, place a higher value on the completion of tasks than on the enhancement of outside relationships and will put in longer hours. This does not mean that they do not like people. It definitely does not mean that they don't like/love their families. It simply means that their self-rating system is wired for work. They will demonstrate their commitment to the people in their life by demonstrating how hard they will work to provide.

Think about some of the people you know who put in long hours. To qualify this, long hours would mean going more than 20% beyond what is required of the person related to hours worked. If 40 hours is the expectation, this person will likely put in 48 or more hours per week. If the person is not as passionate about their job, they will put their hours of effort into other areas. They may put in long hours on a hobby, like working on cars, or building furniture, etc. Their drive to work prohibits them from sitting still too much. They need to be producing something or accomplishing something in order to be happy.

Looking back to the time in life between the ages of 7 and 14, they likely had heroes who made a difference by always being there to work, or putting in long hours to solve a problem. They very likely looked up to a person or character who was diligent in completing the tasks that mattered the most. Again, this could have been a family member, teacher, preacher, coach, or even a fictitious character.

Widow's Peak

A person who has a widow's peak, where the hair tends to come lower in the front center and recedes to the right and left of the center, prefers a relaxed and casual environment. The widow's peak can be a small amount of hair coming down in the center and does not have to have what appears to be hair-loss on the right and left. You will likely notice that they prefer to dress more casual. They often like to work in an environment that is more relaxed as well. Generally, they will prefer to use a first-name basis as they interact with their coworkers, including their bosses and subordinates.

This type of person likely had heroes that were relaxed and relatable. They likely had experiences growing up that taught them how being relaxed and casual sets others at ease and makes the accomplishment of tasks much easier. This person will often prefer to hang out with people who are less formal. They will attend programs that do not require them to dress up more often than they will attend formal programs. They will have a home that is designed for everything to be used as opposed to a formal environment where certain things are off-limits. They want to be relaxed and connected.

Jagged Hairline

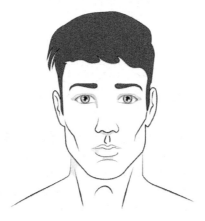

As with all of the other jagged or overly sharp features, this indicates challenges that the person has faced at previous points in their life. In the case of the hairline, as the person is going through the 3 Stages of Psychological development, as defined by Dr. Morris Massey, they likely experienced turmoil and uncertainty. In particular, moving from the imprinting stage (0-6 years old) and through the modeling stage (7-13 years old), the turmoil has a lasting impact on who they are. One of the things you may notice is which side of the forehead is more jagged with the hairline. This is often a subtle difference, but an important one. If the hairline is more jagged on the left, the person had a more tumultuous time in their personal life. If the hairline is more jagged on the right, the person had a more tumultuous time in their school life / external world.

When you realize that the person had a rough childhood, and your see a bump at the very top of the bridge of the nose, you can correlate that around 7 years old was very rough for them. This would mean that they had a rough time and developed defensiveness as a result. Pay attention to the combinations of features, particularly the ones that indicate struggle or challenge. This will open the door for a quick and very deep connection with the person.

Wispy Hair on Either Right or Left Side of Hairline

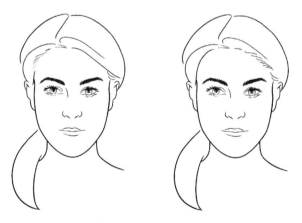

The father's influence shows up in the way we

project ourselves into the world. The mother's influence shows up in the way we interpret the world, or internalize it. Not all influence is good. Not all influence is bad. When a person has wispy hair, generally coupled with the part in their hair, their mother had an influence on the way they internalize their experiences. When it is on the left side, this relates to the internalization of their personal life. When it is on the right side, this relates to the internalization of their professional/educational life.

No Hairline

As you recall, a taller forehead indicates thinking and overthinking. When the forehead is short, it indicates the use of instinct in decision-making, rather than intellect. When there isn't a hairline, it just means that there isn't a hairline. It doesn't actually predict psychological determinations. In order to understand what exists in the mind of that person, you would have to know what their hairline looked like when they did have hair. Keep in mind also that there are medical conditions that cause hair loss. For me, aging seems to be my condition. (insert laugh here)

How a person handles hair loss does say something about them, though. When I was young, one of my heroes was my maternal grandfather. He was bald at an early age and embraced the loss of hair as simply a part of who he was. He didn't cover it up or get offended by it. Instead, he let family members rub his head for luck. He talked about how there were only a certain number of perfect heads made and the rest were covered with hair. He made it fun to be bald. When you look back at previous pictures of a person, before hair loss, you can see what their hairline was. Mine was the widow's peak. I have preferred to dress more casual and to keep my life more casual. Being bald does not really say anything about the person except that their mother's father was also likely bald. This is because the genetics of baldness are passed from the mother's father. My awesome grandsons (which I don't have yet) will have the chance to get great top of the head tans.

8 TEMPERAMENT COMBINATIONS

One of my favorite temperament assessments is the DISC assessment. DISC is an acronym that stands for Dominance, Influence, Steadiness, Conscientiousness. It has been around for quite some time and explains the manner in which we connect with the world very well. One of the things I like about the assessment is that our temperament can change throughout our lives. Typically, once you reach the career of your choice, you will be consistent in your portrayal of self. Each DISC area is simply a portrayal of who a person is as they interact with the world around them. A person can portray themselves differently at home than they do at work. Pay attention to the subtle differences in the shapes of the face from left to right in order to know if the person views the world of work differently than the world of their personal life.

DISC was first introduced as a concept by William Moulton Marston in 1928 in his book, <u>The Emotions</u>

of Normal People. I know, I was thinking the same thing… What is normal? ☺ It wasn't until 1940 that Walter Clark took Marston's theory and put it into practice. He developed the DISC Profile that is still in use today. The idea behind the assessment was to see the manner in which a person portrayed themselves at work. It was also intended to be used to determine if women, in particular, could develop more assertiveness in the workplace. In 2014, I assessed just over 300 people with the DISC assessment and then looked at the variations in their face in order to determine if there was a correlation to the results of their assessment. 9 out of 10, or 90% of the faces correlated to two specific characteristics of the face. The forehead and the chin were the combinations that consistently demonstrated the DISC results of the participants. Let's take a look at what each of the characteristics means, as well as what it looks like.

Dominance, The Competitor

The dominant individual has a combination of a square chin and a rounded forehead. This combination tells us that the person will generally be more focused on the big picture as well as on the task as their primary focus. They will take great pleasure in getting things done and moving the organization forward. This type of person is often described as a "Type A" personality because they are always pushing themselves to higher levels of performance. This type of person has a very high need to achieve, and because of this, they are often ambitious and competitive, striving aggressively to achieve their goals. They are dynamic and adaptable and show a decisiveness and a capacity for direct leadership. They will tend to take charge of situations. They are comfortable with decision-making and prefer to have that level of authority in any relationship.

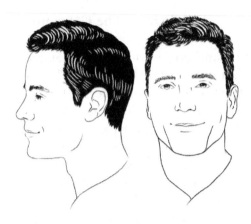

The D: Relating to Others

The emphasis this type of person places on achievement and success significantly affects their relations with other people. In extreme cases, a Competitor can come to treat other people simply as a means to an end, or a way of achieving their personal goals. Dominance is not an emotional factor, and individuals with this type of profile will tend to NOT place great importance on feelings, either their own or others'. The competitive side of Dominance can lead this type of person to see challenges and opposition everywhere, and others sometimes find it difficult to break through this naturally suspicious, skeptical shell.

The D: Common Abilities

We have already seen that the Competitor has qualities of command and leadership. It should be noted, however, that these abilities are based on their direct, demanding nature, and are more suited to structured, formal situations than those where close ties are required.

The Competitor is a competent and confident decision-maker, able to reach a conclusion quickly from minimal information and act accordingly. They are well suited to situations that others would find unbearably stressful, as their desire for challenge and their enjoyment of success against the odds makes them unusually proficient in dealing with such situations. The Competitor is generally adept at handling uncertainty.

The D: Motivating Factors

The Competitor has a strong need to feel in control and will seek opportunities to reinforce and emphasize their personal power. They measure their progress in life by their achievements and successes, and need to maintain a sense of personal momentum.

Being impatient and direct, they do not like having their success in any situations in the hands of another person. They have a strong need to take charge of their future. This type of person will find it unusually difficult to rely on others. They will experience a great deal of frustration when they lose control of situations or if control is taken from them. They are at times prone to wild, impulsive actions in an attempt to relieve the pressure and regain their personal sense of control.

Influence – The Communicator

The person who has Influence as their primary temperament type will have a rounded chin and a round forehead. This type of person is just as big picture as the Dominant person but is driven by relationships over task. They are often seen as the life of the party and love being around others as often as they can be. They are what we know as the classic extrovert. They require greater amounts of external stimulation to feel connected and to feel good about themselves. Back in the days of cameras having film, they were the ones that took pictures of everything, but never developed the film. Today, they will have thousands of pictures on their phone and will likely never do anything with them either. They are fun to be around, better at the start than the finish, and always up for a great conversation or a get-together.

The I/Communicator is just what their name describes. They will have a stronger need for interacting with others on a personal level. They will lag behind at parties and gatherings catching up with as many people as they can. The Influencer profile can be very closely linked with those styles that interact easily and fluently with others. This type of individual will be confident in social settings, even if they are unfamiliar with the rest of the members of that setting. They will seek out ways to draw attention to themselves and will enjoy personal compliments more than the other types. They thrive on creating positive relationships with others.

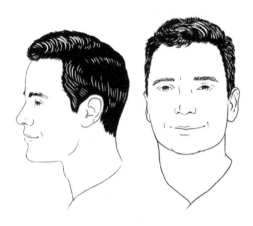

The I: Relating to Others

Relating to others is what a Communicator does best. They are open to others and confident in their own social abilities, allowing them to interact positively in almost any situation. Their strong and evident confidence, coupled with their genuine interest in the ideas and especially feelings of other people, are often found charming by those around them. The Communicator profile represents a person who not just wants, but needs to know how others are doing.

The I: Common Abilities

As you are now aware, communication is the strong suit of this type of person. They tend to be very good persuaders and even better charmers. The Communicator has a keen ability to read other people and understand both what is being said verbally and what is being communicated nonverbally. They are very comfortable with change and seek ways to keep things fun and exciting.

The I: Motivating Factors

Communicators are motivated by relations with others. Specifically, they need to feel accepted by those around them. They react poorly if they perceive themselves to be rejected or disliked. Praise and approval make a strong impression on them, and they will sometimes go to great lengths to achieve this kind of reaction from other people.

Especially important to this type of person are the opinions and reactions of their particularly close friends. When a Communicator develops very close ties with somebody, that person becomes part of their 'Influence Group', as it is known. Their actions will often be designed to improve and extend relations within this group, even to the extent of alienating people who are not part of this circle. This factor can make Communicators appear unpredictable at times.

Steady, AKA The Cooperator

The Steady person will have a round chin and a flat forehead. They are more on the cautious and detailed side of life than the D or the I. They judge themselves based on how calm their relationships are and tend to measure their day by how calm they are able to keep the things in their life. They like for things to be right, need time to make decisions, need more time for change, and do incredibly well at working behind the scenes. They are not seeking the spotlight, but rather consistency in their work. They avoid conflict whenever possible and pursue consensus with coworkers as well as with their family.

The Steady profile used to be less common than the other types until the Millennial Generation entered the scene. The Cooperator maintains a balance between tasks and relationships. They will come across as steady, calm, patient, gentle, and open. They are generally agreeable and warm-hearted, being sympathetic to others' points of view and valuing positive interaction with others. They are not outgoing by nature, however, and rely on other, more assertive, people to take the lead.

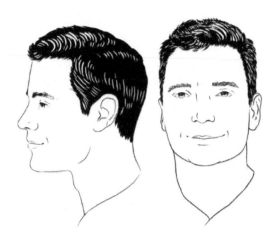

The S: Relating to Others

As in their general lifestyle, this type of person will look to more socially assertive people to initiate relationships of any kind - their solid, dependable outlook makes them far more suited to the maintenance of interpersonal relations than making initial contact. For this reason, their circle of friends and close acquaintances is often small but tightly-knit.

The S: Common Abilities

The Cooperator's core strengths can be summarized as supportive. They are dependable and loyal. This combines with an emotional literacy to make them particularly effective listeners and counselors. They are also unusually persistent in their approach, having the patience and restraint to work steadily at a task until it is achieved. This makes them unusually capable of dealing with laborious tasks that many other styles would simply not have the patience to complete.

The S: Motivating Factors

The underlying patience of this type of person is the root of their motivating factors. They need to feel that they have the support of those around them and, more importantly, time to adapt to new situations. They have an inherent dislike of change and will prefer to maintain the *status quo* whenever possible. Sudden alterations in their circumstances can be very difficult for them to deal with.

Once engaged on a task, they prefer to concentrate on just that task until it is complete. Interruptions and distractions of any kind can be particularly demotivating in these situations.

Conscientious, AKA The Coordinator

The Conscientious person, also known as the Coordinator, will have a square chin and a flat forehead. They are great at details and are often the ones that will coordinate the manner in which work is to be done. They come across as cautious and skeptical and prefer to deal with things that can be proven rather than with things that are theoretical. They are masters of process management, but sometimes forget about the end result in their quest to ensure that things are done just right. They are often misunderstood in their communication because they tend to question things as well as people. This questioning can come across as untrusting or as being irritated. In reality, they are simply trying to ensure that they have a full grasp on the situation.

The Coordinator is passive by nature. They have a tendency to come across as distant or uninterested. This can be interpreted by others as being cold or uncaring. The Coordinator will often be reluctant to share information about themselves. This is not a dislike for others, but a reserved nature because of their strong need for control of situations. The Conscientious person is just as ambitious as the Dominant person, they simply have more struggles with opening up and sharing their desires for success. The C does not particularly care for conflict, but has such a strong need for rules and order that they will jump into conflict situations in order to preserve that order.

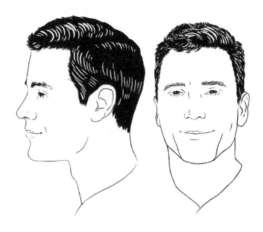

The C: Relating to Others

The Coordinator has many strengths, but the ability to relate easily to other people is rarely a top strength. The combination of a passive social style with a strong suspiciousness makes it difficult for this type of person to form or maintain close relationships. Their friendships or close acquaintances will normally be based on mutual interests or common aims, rather than emotional considerations. They will tend to relate on logical, rather than emotional appeals.

The C: Common Abilities

Coordinators are generally very self-reliant people. They tend to run ideas by others with the desire for others to simply affirm that they are right. They have structured ways of thinking and often show particular strengths when it comes to organizing facts or working with precise detail or systems. They are great at logical problem solving, working with facts and figures, and organizing. They have a tendency to not offer their ideas and solutions, however, unless they are directly asked for them.

The C: Motivating Factors

There is one factor that has a more significant effect on a Coordinator's motivation than any other - certainty. They need to feel completely sure of their position, and of others' expectations of them, before they are able to proceed. Because of this, they have a very strong aversion to risk and will rarely take any action unless they can feel absolutely sure about its outcomes. They do well when predictability and a sense of control are present.

9 COMBINATIONS OF CHARACTERISTICS

This chapter will be a lot of fun. I went through and asked a number of people to tell me about people they would like to be able to predict. The result is the combinations listed in the chapter. I think you will have fun reading about the different types of people as well as discovering how you can know which character you are about to interact with from the moment you meet a person.

The full story of a person's face is in the combination of characteristics. Each individual characteristic, on its own, doesn't tell you much about the person. Even from the temperament standpoint, by looking at four characteristics of the face together, you can tell what the secondary temperament characteristic is. I want to take you through a few of my favorite combinations that will amaze the people whom you are interacting with, and that will set you apart as a bit of a guru in the communication world.

My Favorite Combinations of characteristics...

- The Broken Heart in College Combination
  - When a person has an up and down line on the end of their nose in combination with a notch on their left ear at the 20 to 22 year-old mark (just back from the top of the outer ear fold), this would indicate that they fell in love and had their heart broken around 20-22 years old. Look at the left ear on the left hand picture and the line on the end of the nose in the right picture.

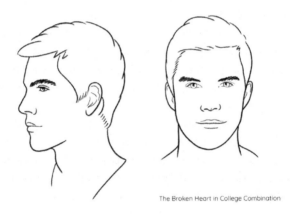

The Broken Heart in College Combination

- The Sorry About High School Combination
  - When a person has a bump a little less than half-way down from the top of the nose ridge in combination with notch on the right ear just barely up from the start of the top of the outer ear fold (where the ear starts to leave the top side of the face), they had a hard time their freshman year of high school.

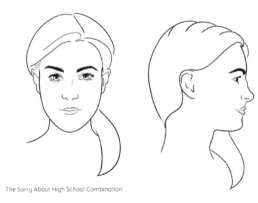

The Sorry About High School Combination

- The I Will Never Be Like My Parents Combination
  - When a person has a bump half way up or higher on the bridge of the nose, has a single vertical line in between the eyebrows, and has a notch at the top of the left ear, they went a different direction than their parents, have some defensiveness, and their personal life changed at 18.

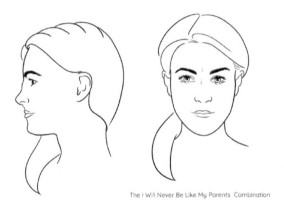

The I Will Never Be Like My Parents Combination

- The Pay Attention To Me Now Combination
    - When a person has eyes that seem to come out from the eye socket, they have a short upper lip (length of upper lip from mouth to nose), and a line on their chin (between the lower lip and start of the jaw line) that looks like the top half of a circle, they want attention now and need to hear good things about themselves.

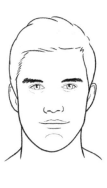

The Pay Attention To Me Now Combination

- The Incredibly Determined Combination
  - o When the person has a wider lower jawline, a square chin, flat eyebrows, a bulge (will pad) between the eyebrows, and has a wider nose bridge (width of the bridge of the nose horizontally), they are incredibly determined to get things done and to do them their own way.

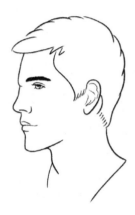
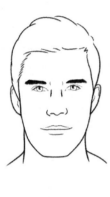

The Incredibly Determined Combination

- The I Just Want Us All To Be Happy Combination
  - When a person has a rounded and full face, a rounded chin, a rounded hairline, and a flat forehead, they want peace and harmony and for everyone to just be happy. You will also notice an arch in the eyebrows which reveals their compulsion to keep things under control.

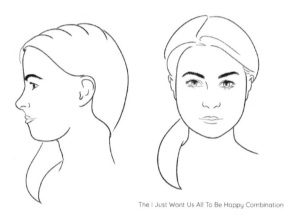

The I Just Want Us All To Be Happy Combination

- The I Came To Have Some Fun Combination
  - When a person has a rounded chin, a rounded forehead, rounded eyebrows with no arch and that tuck under the brow ridge on the inside, and folded back ears, they love to feel engaged and enjoy a great party. Pay attention to the eyebrows in this picture versus the one right before it.

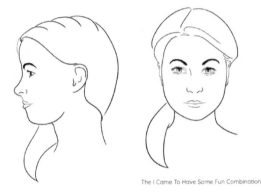

The I Came To Have Some Fun Combination

- The Let's Get Some Things Done Before We Have Fun Combination
    - When a person has a square chin, rounded forehead, flat eyebrows, and a wider jaw line, they want to get all the work done before they have fun.

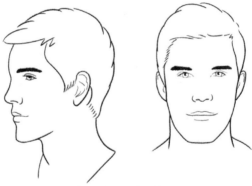

The Let's Get Some Things Done Before We Have Fun Combination

- The Let's Not Joke Around Combination
  - When a person has a flat forehead, square chin, flat eyebrows, three vertical lines between the eyebrows when they pull their eyebrows together, eyes that sit back in the eye sockets, a small mouth, and a square hairline, they don't want to joke around. They want to get stuff done and get it done right.

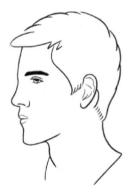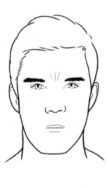

The Let's Not Joke Around Combination

- The This Person Creeps Me Out Combination
    - When a person has a shorter forehead, eyes that have the top half of the iris cut off by the upper eye lid, a pointed chin, angular cheekbones, and unusually small ears, this is the type of person that creeps me out a bit. The reason for this is that they use their instincts (forehead), have violent tendencies (top of the iris cut off), are self-centered (chin), react sharply (cheekbones), and have neurological issues (ears).

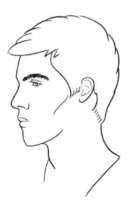
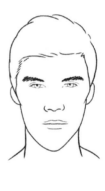

The This Person Creeps Me Out Combination

- The I Am Good At Sports/Winning Combination
  - When a person has a square chin, round forehead, thick eyebrows that are flat, strongly folded back ears, and wide jaw line, they will be a tremendous competitor. They will also not likely be able to quit until they win.

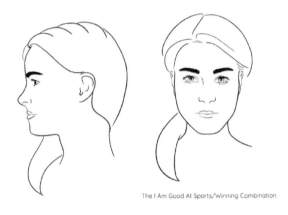

The I Am Good At Sports/Winning Combination

- The Please Don't Confront Me Combination
  - When a person has a round chin and a flat forehead, as well as nostrils that suck in (are very small), and their ear lobe seems to come out from their head at the bottom.

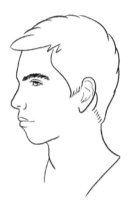 

The Please Don't Confront Me Combination

- The Let's Get Some Things Done Before We Have Fun Combination
    - When a person has a square chin, rounded forehead, flat eyebrows, and a wider jaw line, they want to get all the work done before they have fun.

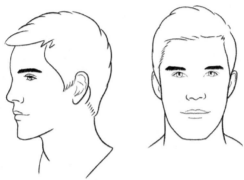

The Let's Get Some Things Done Before We Have Fun Combination

- The Are All People Really That Dumb Combination
  - When a person has a taller forehead, eyebrows that seem to grow together, a round forehead and a square chin, they will be more quick to judge others around them and will often think that other people "just don't get it."

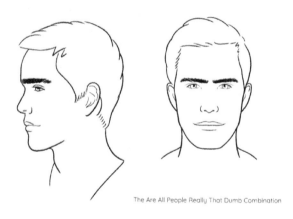

The Are All People Really That Dumb Combination

- The Anal Retentive Combination, Just Do It Myself Combination and Now I Am Worn Out
  - When a person has a taller forehead that is flat across, a square chin, larger ears that do not fold back, and bags under their eyes, they will try to delegate, but will end up taking things back. This person will often wear themselves out doing things themselves because they have such a strong need to make sure that they are done right.

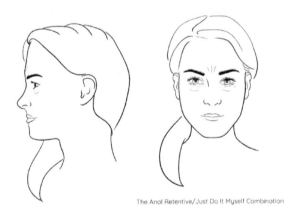

The Anal Retentive/Just Do It Myself Combination

- The Seriously… You Can't Figure This Out On Your Own Combination
  - When a person has a taller forehead, eyebrows that seem to grow together, and ears that look like they are tilted back (angled differently than most), they will wonder why others can't figure out the same things that they have figured out. The angled ears demonstrate that they process the world differently than most people around them.

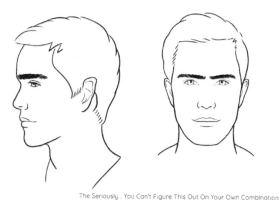

The Seriously... You Can't Figure This Out On Your Own Combination

- The I'm Okay As Long as There Are Rules Combination
  - When a person has a square chin, a pronounced brow ridge, and a flat forehead, they like to work with rules and systems and prefers to simply work in the background until they get the job done.

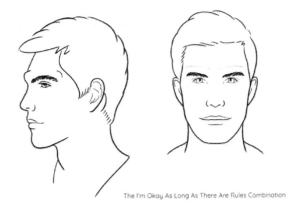

The I'm Okay As Long As There Are Rules Combination

- The All My Friends Know I've Got This Combination
  - When a person has a round forehead, a square chin, a vertical line in the center of the chin, ears that fold back, flat eyebrows, a gum line that shows, and strong horizontal lines across the forehead that do not have a break in them, this is the type of person that is determined, driven by their goals, feels into their accomplishments, and doesn't give up until they complete the task. All their friends know that they have things under control.

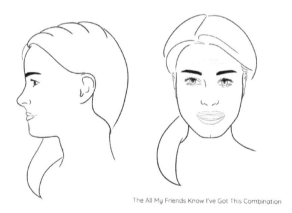

The All My Friends Know I've Got This Combination

Requested Combinations

The following were submitted by people that I reached out to about combinations that would be of interest to them. I had a lot of fun going through the characteristics and outlining the facial structure of these specific types of people. I wrote out the combinations slightly different on the rest of these to explain why each characteristic was important.

- The Ultimate Babysitter Combination
  - A great babysitter is relational (round chin), logical (flat forehead), driven by mission (septum of the nose is lower than the outside edges of the nostrils), hairline is square (can work long hours and stay focused), and they have a rounded area like a ball on the end of their nose (likes to always know what is going on).

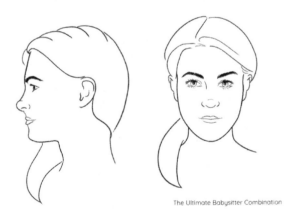

The Ultimate Babysitter Combination

- The Excellent With Money Combination
  - There are two specific characteristics that relate to money and a couple of other characteristics that have a strong impact on how money is handled. When a person has a larger nose as compared to their face (is good at handling money), three horizontal lines on their forehead that go all the way across (is good at earning money), has a taller upper lip from the lip to the nose (is good with delayed gratification), and nostrils you cannot see into when they are looking straight at you (better with budgeting time and money), then this person will attract, keep, budget, and be patient with their accumulation of money. As an example, seeing into nostrils when a person is looking at you means that it appears that the nostrils flare up in the front, making it possible to see into the edge of the nose.

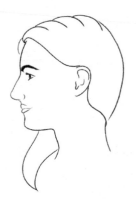
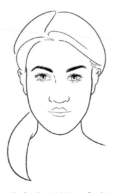

The Excellent With Money Combination

- The Great Car Salesperson Combination
  - Most successful salespeople are either D's or I's on the DISC temperament assessment. It isn't that the other types can't sell, but a combination of these two makes the person relational, approachable, and driven to succeed. When a person has a rounded forehead, a chin that is in between rounded and squared, you cannot see into their nostrils when they are looking straight at you (good with budgeting time and money), and they have a wider jaw structure below their ears (persistent and doesn't quit), they will be a great car salesperson.

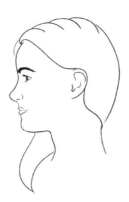

The Great Car Salesperson Combination

- The Machiavellian Narcissist Combination
  - This person will have a pointed chin (judges themselves only on their own thoughts), a round forehead (emotional decision making), folded back ears (action and emotion mental processing), and angular features to their face, particularly the cheekbone areas (sharp and quick reactions to others).

The Machiavellian Narcissist Combination

- The Don't Play Poker With This Person Combination
  - Poker players are risk takers. The one's that win the most often have a rounded forehead (emotional decision-maker), smaller ears (visual processor – better at reading the tell of another person), square chin (driven by goals and accomplishments), and a wider jaw (back of the jaw where the jaw hinges – doesn't give up)

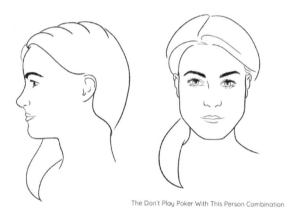

The Don't Play Poker With This Person Combination

- The I'm Always A Victim Combination
  - Those who see themselves as victims have a few characteristics in common. They tend to be emotional decision-makers (round forehead), judge themselves by either relations or just self (either rounded chin or pointed chin), they believe bad things are going to happen (their eyes angle down from the inside corner to the outside corner), and they have unresolved emotional issues (bags under their eyes). As a side note, some people have bags under their eyes because of a vitamin deficiency instead of emotional issues that have not been resolved.

 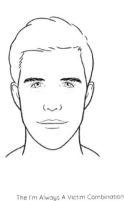

The I'm Always A Victim Combination

- The I'm Always Right And You Are Wrong Combination
    - This type of person has no inner ear ridge on either ear. This indicates an inability to see where they could be wrong. If they have no inner ear ridge on the right, they can't see where they would be wrong at work. If it is on the left, they can't see where they would be wrong at home. If it is both side, they simply can't see how they could be wrong.

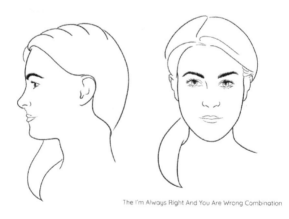

The I'm Always Right And You Are Wrong Combination

- The Let's Argue Combination
  - o This person has a forehead that seems to tilt forward (mentally aggressive), thicker eyebrows (projects their thoughts and feelings on others), and has no inner ear ridge (can't see that they could be wrong)

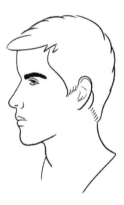
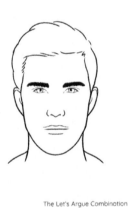

The Let's Argue Combination

- The If I Ain't Happy, Ain't Nobody Happy Combination
    - This type of person has a flat forehead (logical processor), a square chin (driven by tasks and goals), angled down eyes (sees bad before good), and a small or no inner ear ridge (can't see that they could be wrong). This type of person is generally skeptical and has a strong need to be right.

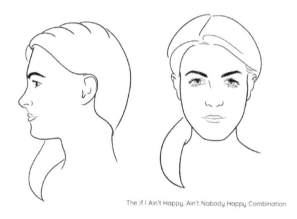

The If I Ain't Happy, Ain't Nobody Happy Combination

- The I Want To Be Included Every Time Combination
  - When a person has a nose that sticks out further than normal for the size of their face, not wide but long, (sticks their nose into other people's business) and they have a ball or rounded area on the end of their nose (likes to be kept in the loop at all times), they will continuously try to get involved in other people's business and want to always know what is going on.

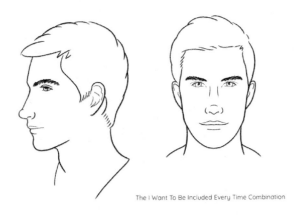

The I Want To Be Included Every Time Combination

- The I Just Can't Admit My Age Combination
  - When a person has no lines on their face (generally removed through the use of Botox), has a rounded forehead (emotional decision-maker), and has a rounded chin (judges themselves based on what they think others think of them), they will struggle to admit their age or accept that they are aging.

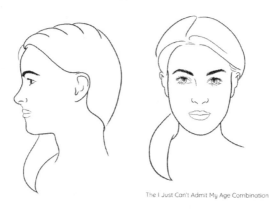

The I Just Can't Admit My Age Combination

- The Have To Prove My Point / First Of All... Combination
  - When a person has a rounded forehead that seems to bulge forward (aggressive and emotional decision-maker), a small area just above and between the eyebrows that bulges out when they furrow their brow (strong will pad), their eyebrows are thicker (projects their thoughts and emotions onto others), and a wider mouth (more boisterous or loud), they will be the type of person that has to prove their point and will begin their sentences with something like... First of All!

The Have To Prove My Point Combination

- The Not Going To Date My Daughter Combination
  - When a young man is a teenager and has three lines that look like the outside of a circle just outside of both sides of their mouth (uses depressants like marijuana or lots of drinking), has a rounded forehead (emotional decision-maker), a shorter forehead (street smarts instead of intellect), has ripples in their jaw line (overly aggressive), a short upper lip (not patience or no capacity for delayed gratification), the top half of their iris is blocked by their upper eyelid (violent tendencies), they are definitely not going to date my daughter!

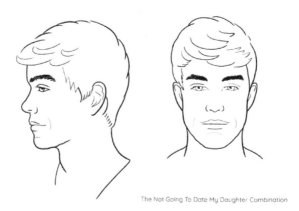

The Not Going To Date My Daughter Combination

- The Slowly Dying Inside Because I Keep Conforming Combination
  - Most people who conform have either a rounded forehead and rounded chin or a flat forehead and rounded chin. The rounded chin indicates judging themselves based on what others would think of them. They also tend to have a strong inner ear ridge (strong sense of what others think of them and that they could have the wrong perspective), and tend to have their upper eyelids overlapping or folded over (takes on too much and then takes on more). This person is just worn out from trying to do their own thing without getting the approval and collaboration they thought they would get.

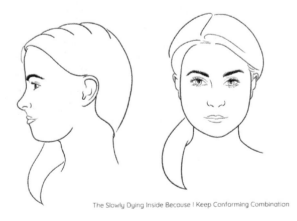

The Slowly Dying Inside Because I Keep Conforming Combination

- The Never Going To Buy and Never Going To Say No Either Combination
  - This type of person has a rounded chin and a flat forehead (S temperament combination), a tall forehead (overthinks), strong inner ear ridges (aware that they might have the wrong perspective), a line on their chin (likes affirmation), and their nostrils tend to suck in (insecure about their life). This leads them to want to make others happy and to not be secure enough in who they are to tell the other person no on a product or service that they are trying to sell. It also keeps them from saying yes because they are worried about being wrong either direction.

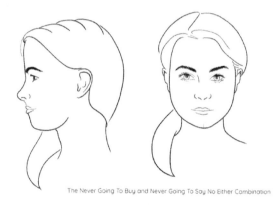

The Never Going To Buy and Never Going To Say No Either Combination

The combinations have been a lot of fun to put together. After reading the book, if there is a combination that was not covered that you would like to know about. Reach out on Facebook or through my website. My business Facebook page is at:

https://www.facebook.com/jodyhollandtraining/

My website is: http://www.jodyholland.com

If you are interested in receiving tips on Leadership every Monday morning… Text: jody   To: 66866

10 SITUATIONAL CONTEXTS

Lots of people have participated in personality assessments, strength assessments, temperament assessments and the like. These tools are great, and they reveal a great deal about who a person is. I have loved assessments for more than 20 years now and have found them to be very valuable in hiring, coaching, training, and the overall development of people. The only problem that I have with an assessment is that people don't tend to carry their results around for the rest of the world to see. I would love it if people simply wore a badge that said, "I am an INTJ" or "ENFP" or if they outlined the Clifton Strengths® or their DISC profile pattern. If that were always available when you first meet a person, we would have a much easier time in discovering how we can connect at a deep level with the person. The problem is… I can't meet a person and ask them to take a quick 15-60 minute test, depending on the test, before I interact with them. This would be completely impractical. And, it might come across as a little weird for me to ask every person that I meet to take a test before I was willing to interact with them. That is the very reason why learning to read faces is so critically important. If I know how to read a person before they even finish shaking my hand, I have given myself an incredible advantage! I have stacked the deck in my favor when it comes to sales, service, leadership, parenting, building relationships with coworkers, finding love, or any other aspect of human interaction. I don't know about you, but I really like to have all of the advantages that I can! I want the odds to forever be in my favor.

As you think about the different areas that you might use face reading, think about it from the angle of relationship building. Think about how relationships make everything work. The world's problems can be broken down in to either people problems or systems problems. Face reading is a system to eliminate people problems. I look forward to helping you apply the skills you have acquired and will continue to build in making relationships better, deeper, and more fulfilling through face reading

Leadership

John Maxwell described leadership as "influence." As a leader, whether in your own company or working for an organization, your primary role is to develop influence with those whom you are responsible for leading. Your level of influence will determine your level of success in life. With the use of face reading, it is like having an instant personality test for anyone and everyone that you meet. You can visit with an employee and know right then how to adapt to their communication needs. You can deal with tough situations and know how to adapt your approach to the person or persons that you are with based on whether or not they are defensive, whether they respond to logic or emotion, whether they judge themselves based on goals or based on relationships. Knowing this information sets you apart in the direct interactions you will have with others.

As a leader, your primary role is to inspire action in others. Leadership is one to many. Management is one to one. As a leader, the more you understand the thought patterns of those you are leading, the easier it becomes to accommodate for the multiple needs that might be in the room. You will also begin to notice patterns within the different levels of authority that work for you. For example, there will be a more common temperament and a more common self-reflection style for people who are at the executive level. The same is true at the manager level, the supervisor level, as well as for the entry-level employee. This is not to say that each person is in the role that they will be in forever. What you will notice is that as people begin to shift their way of thinking when they desire to move up, they will also have subtle shifts in the structure of their face. They will change things about the way they project themselves into the world as well as the way they evaluate themselves within that world of work.

Use this science to help you establish relationships more quickly, more deeply, and more effortlessly, and you will find that others become drawn to you. Your ability to connect and inspire others is what is often referred to as your magnetism. Charisma is not the same thing as magnetism. Magnetism goes beyond being just inspired. It also moves that person to seek out ways to support you and build you up. It moves them to look for ways to draw other performers into the organization. It moves them to seek out ways of impressing you through their increased efforts. Your role as a leader ultimately comes down to your ability to motivate others to do the necessary work. When they have the motivation/desire to perform at their best, then your job as a leader becomes more fulfilling as well as quite a bit easier.

Executive Coaching and Life Coaching

Over the last couple of decades, I have had the opportunity to coach over 300 executives directly. I have worked with multiple industries, from healthcare to finance to manufacturing and food production, to retail, restaurants, and professional service firms. In working with those industries, one of the things that typically holds an executive coach or a life coach back is learning the industry jargon. Knowing the industry jargon is what is commonly used to create a connection with the leader that is being coached. When you master the science of face reading, you give yourself an incredible advantage over other coaches. The person who can read faces can connect without the need for memorizing the industry terms. They know things about a person before the conversation even begins.

In my online program on face reading, I go into detail on what the key connection triggers are and how to use them to build instant rapport with anyone. The use of these connection triggers help the other person to feel at ease with you and to open up about what is really going on. Additionally, when the person knows that you already know a great deal about them, they are much less likely to try to fool you. When I start with a quick face reading before the first session begins, people's eyes get bigger in surprise that a person could know that much about them. Then, they say something to the effect of, "there's no use in trying to fool you because you know me better than anyone that I work with." This type of statement sets the tone in their mind that they need to pay attention and be completely honest. This approach reduces the amount of time it takes to get to a positive breakthrough by as much as 75%. Since I began using face reading in my executive and life coaching sessions, I have been able to realign a person's beliefs, thoughts, actions, and results typically in 3 to 4 sessions. Before face reading, it would typically take a year of work with a person every month to achieve the same results.

Hiring

Have you ever hired someone that you ended up wishing you had never met? Most people who have been in management or leadership roles for more than a year have hired at least one person that they regretted ever meeting. This experience is fairly common, but it is also preventable. When a person interviews, they typically look for whether or not they like the person. At a subconscious level, we are continuously comparing ourselves to that person and determining how like us they are. We tend to hire people that are just like us. The mistake in this is that we are not hiring for our position, at least not most of the time. Instead, we are hiring for a position that would report to us. We want to get along with the person that we hire, but the real reason is to find the person who can do the job, will do the job, and will do it the way that we need it done. I read an article a few years back in the Harvard Business Review that indicated that using a predictive hiring system will typically produce a good hiring rate of 14%. That means that 86% of the hires will prove to be bad ideas if we don't have additional insights about the person we are interviewing!

Most people believe they are great at determining whether a person can and will do the job. Yet, those same people typically have a bad record of hires. When you use face reading as a part of the hiring process, you can find the profile of the kind of person whom you want without the emotional and ego-driven interference that typically accompanies the process. If you need a logical person who will think through things and will operate with meticulous details, you look for those characteristics on their face. That profile is flat forehead, tall forehead, square chin, and three vertical lines between the eyebrows. If you need a person that will push forward no matter what, then you need a person with a square chin, round forehead that tilts slightly forward, flat across eyebrows, straight horizontal lines across the forehead, and a wide jaw line. The combinations that you look for are simply revealing who a person is. As much as 85% of resume's will have exaggerated information on them. Very few people ever walk into an interview and tell you what their real weaknesses are. They practice their responses. Well, if they are any good, they practice. The use of this science levels the playing field and helps to ensure that you hire the person who is right for the job. This benefits the company because they get the right person, and it greatly benefits the person because you are setting them up for success!

Sales

When pursuing a career in sales, the use of face reading gives us an edge in building the trust that we need with our prospect. The challenge that many people have in using face reading for sales is that they try to manipulate the other person. That was not and is not the intent of using face reading. The objective is to learn to map out the communication and emotional preferences of a prospect and then to adapt our style to meet theirs. People like people who are similar. Within the brain, we have what is known as mirror neurons. Their neurons are seeking ways to mimic the person whom we are with. When the person is already quite a bit like us, it is very easy to mimic them. This allows the conscious mind to relax and to allow some of its defense mechanisms to take a break. This is what is known as bypassing the critical factor of the mind. If a person is too different from us, we tend to stimulate our defense mechanisms in order to protect ourselves from potential danger.

When selling to others, even if you have simply been able to find their profile picture through social media, you will know how to adapt your approach in order to fit the person's needs. You will also know how to adjust your proposal to fit the needs of the person whom you will be presenting to. If you have someone with a square chin, round forehead, flat eyebrows, and smaller ears, you will want to have a short proposal that is colorful and has a chart, or great graphics. This will appeal to who the person is and generate more trust from them to you. If the person has flat eyebrows, flat forehead, square chin, larger ears and eyes that set back in their head, you will want to add lots of details. You will also want to be prepared with references if they request them. Additionally, it is best NOT to try to hard close this person. They need time to think through things and make sense of them on their own.

Use face reading in order to adapt your...
- Style of communication
- Proposal style
- Presentation style
- Closing style
- Follow up style

I encourage you to pay close attention to the chapter on temperaments in order to have a strong basis for how you adapt yourself to the person whom you are with at the time.

For more information on how to increase your effectiveness in sales, check out my books on sales.

Hypnotic Selling: http://bit.ly/hypnoticbook
Selling With Honor: http://bit.ly/sellinghonor

Creating a Client or Donor Profile

One of the more engaging contracts I have gotten is that of profiling the people who are likely to buy from a specific company. After this contract, I received a contract to profile donors who would likely give to a certain cause. I have done this a number of times for both for-profit and not-for-profit organizations over the last several years. In creating a profile of the right person to target, I simply had to go back through the pictures of the people who have bought or donated in the past. There are profiles of people who are highly likely to purchase from you, and there are profiles of people that it will take years for you to close. Once you begin to understand the characteristics and what each characteristic means, it becomes easier to create your own profile of a great client or a great donor.

Many donors are driven by a desire to fulfill a mission, which is indicated in the septum of the nose being lower than the outside edges of the nostrils. Many people who buy for technical reasons such as higher quality or longer-lasting products will have a flat forehead, medium height, square chin, and eyes that are more deep-set in the head. Regardless of what you are selling or raising money for, you need to know the common characteristics of the people that believe in your product or mission. Gone are the days of "spray and pray," which is the model of spraying out your information to everyone that you can think of and praying that something sticks. This methodology is frustrating to both the person sending it out as well as to the person being blasted with it. Take the top 20 supporters of your cause or your product and begin to look for common characteristics. So far, I have always been able to find 3 to 5 characteristics that are the same on the faces of every top supporter. This doesn't work if you take 20 random customers. It has to be the top 20. After all, we are not seeking people who may or may not support us. Instead, we are seeking people who have the highest likelihood of supporting us. That is what sets us apart from everyone else. It is also what makes our lives as fundraisers, marketers, or sales reps much easier. Develop your incredible advantage by mastering the science of face reading! There is a section in my online program on how to profile a person as a great client or a great donor.

Managing and Resolving Conflict

Conflict consumes close to 20% of the working hours of a typical manager or leader. This can be conflict between the manager/leader and another person or conflict that the manager/leader has to get involved with to resolve between two or more other people. This means that one day, full-time, every week is spent resolving conflict in one way or another. The reason that conflict exists is because of a clash of either needs or values. Either way, the conflict is based on seeing the world differently than the person whom we are in conflict with. By learning how to quickly adapt your communication style to the person whom you are with, you are best prepared to calm the situation down. You have the ability to understand who the person is and what they are really saying in order to pull them in a better direction. When we push on a person, they typically push back. When we connect and then guide them, they typically follow.

In my book, <u>Yay! I'm A Supervisor! Now What!?</u>, I have a full chapter on the communication strategies to resolve conflict. The model I developed is the B-FIRM model. It is an acronym that stands for Behavior, Feeling, Impact, Reflective listening, and My expectations. When we deal with behaviors instead of making conflict personal, we lower the emotional temperature of the person we are confronting. By understanding the likely reactive pattern of the person, we can present our message in the best manner possible. Within communication, 93% of what we interpret from the messages of others is based on non-verbal cues. Tone of voice, body language, and facial expressions make up that 93%. By presenting in a way that is disarming to that particular person, we calm them down, connect with them, and direct them toward a win-win agreement.

Working Well With Others

Everything you learned up to this point was to set you up to work well with others. You must first understand who you are and your likely reaction and response patterns before you can fully understand others. When you think about how you work with others, it will ultimately come down to how you connect with others. Your connection to others is based on your projection of self. I would encourage you to take some time and stare at your face in the mirror. What do you see? What do you feel? If that was the person whom you were going to interact with effectively, what would your strategy be? When we begin to evaluate ourselves in the same manner that we would another person, we begin to grasp what others are seeing in us. It takes a great deal of self-awareness to become effective at interacting with others. When we master who we are, we can master our communication with others.

Make sure that you take the time to review the quick reference guide (last chapter) as well as re-read the book. Practice with one characteristic at a time. For example, focus on people's forehead for an entire day and see if you can master predicting if they are emotional or logical decision makers. The ultimate connection with others is when you begin to put 3, 4, and 5 different characteristics of their face together all at once. This is when the story of who they are really comes to light.

Parenting

There are so many applications within parenting for the use of face reading. Once your child reaches about 2 years old, you will begin to see characteristics on their face that are predictive of the behavior patterns. As your child grows, you will notice there will be subtle, and sometimes significant, changes in the structure of their face. Pay attention to these changes because it will open up the door for conversation with your child. It will help you to understand what they are going through and how you can connect with them to help them.

Another application of face reading in parenting is to master the art of reading who their friends are. In today's social media driven world, it is incredibly easy to find pictures of your child's friends. By doing some online recon work, you can discover the overall makeup of the people they are hanging out with and then help guide them to be with friends who will build them up. One of the things I did not outline about noses in the previous chapters is that of knowing when a person…

- Sticks their nose in other people's business
  - This type of nose will be one that sticks out further from the person's face than normal. An abnormally extended nose is indicative of one who will be looking into what everyone else is doing. If they have the ball on the end of the nose in combination with the nose that sticks out more, they will also be a gossip.
- Is treacherous
  - When a person's nose seems to extend out at the very end and then tip down, this person can often be treacherous in relationships. Think about a more subtle version of how a witch's nose would look from a kid's movie. That is one to watch out for.

Finding Love

We are often attracted to a specific structure of the face. We may not have consciously processed what facial components are the most attractive to us, but we are being swayed by the ears, or nose, or jaw line, or some combination of aspects about a person's face. If we are attracted to something that is not good for us, we need to intentionally look for the components that will support us. As an example, people with a square chin and rounded forehead are often attracted to the same two facial features. When you have two D temperaments in the relationship, there is normally a power struggle for who gets to be in charge.

The key to using face reading to build your relationships is in finding the features that compliment who you are. You need to find a person who fills in the gaps that exist for you. The good news is that the other person needs the same thing. They are needing someone who "completes them" as well. One of the keys to great relationships is balance. Face reading is a fantastic vehicle to predict balance before you even go on the first date. With all of the online dating systems out there, simply look for facial features instead of the best selfie, and you significantly increase your odds of finding love.

Enhancing The Learning Process

Every person we develop within our businesses has a specific learning model, aspects of who they are that motivate them, and a manner in which they judge themselves. By knowing these three primary areas, we are best prepared to transfer knowledge to others. Imagine being able to design a learning experience where people would have the highest likelihood of mastering the information being presented. When we study the ear structure of a person, we get a clear picture of how the person processes and recalls information. By understanding their decision-making models, we are best prepared to use the right triggers and affirmation in our teaching to stimulate their desire to learn. And finally, by know how a person judges themselves in combination with their decision-making, we know what their drivers for learning would be.

One of the most common mistakes we make is to assume all students process information in the same manner. Whether your students are adults or youth, you still need to master adapting to their style of learning. This adaptation provides a deeper connection between the material and the student. When you are in a room full of different styles of learning, it also helps to understand how to adapt your messaging to ensure that other people are internalizing the. Face reading helps you adapt to each student and to become more effective at asking them questions that will help them demonstrate their knowledge. Many times, the kinesthetic processor will suffer in a standard meeting because they learn by doing and feeling instead of by listening or reading. Each instructor needs to adapt their teaching strategies to fit the needs of their class as well as to tap into the learning styles of struggling students.

Staying In Love

As a person who has managed to stay married for a quarter of a century, I can say that mastering the science of face-reading has helped me to adapt to the needs of my wife. By understanding how she is processing information as well as learning the history of her psychological journey, I have become a neuro-hacker in the relationship. She is an incredibly brilliant woman, but I needed to know what I could do to adapt to her specific needs. Face reading has helped me to understand her love language, her thought process, and her motivation. These are key aspects to understanding what I can do to meet her needs and strengthen the relationship.

Without face reading, I believe we would struggle quite a bit more because I would be guessing as to what was going on in her mind when we communicated. I am not a mind reader, but as a face reader I am a great connector. If you find that your relationship needs to be deepened or needs a boost in its connection, this is the perfect vehicle to ensure that you stay as connected as possible with the one you love. It also helps you to understand what has been going wrong if you are in struggle. Most of the struggles in relationships are related to not connecting deep enough or often enough. Most of that is dependent on each person's ability to communicate effectively and articulate their needs. Learn to read faces and you learn to connect hearts.

Coaching Sports

Whether you are coaching small children, high-schoolers, college athletes, or adults, you need to know how to get into the head of the athlete. Dennis Waitley in his book, The Psychology of Winning, describes the difference between a 1st place, 2nd place, and 3rd place winner in the Olympics as simply a difference in their thoughts. A person's thought patterns are driven by their beliefs. Their thoughts then generate specific actions, which generate outcomes. Regardless of the level of competition, when you are able to hack into the neurological patterns of an athlete, you can help set them up for greater success!

It is critical to understand how a person judges themselves as an athlete. It is also critical to understand how they process information and how they are motivated to perform. You will need to pay attention to their forehead, their chin, their jaw structure, and to any defensiveness (bridge of the nose) and insecurities (narrowed nostrils) in order to help move them to success. Throughout history, many coaches simply yell louder and push harder in order to get their athletes to perform. The new model of face reading (neuro-hacking) gives the coach a tremendous advantage in pushing their athletes and teams to greater levels of success. By adapting their strategies for achieving performance outcomes, they set themselves and their team up to win more often and dominate in their given fields.

Understanding Self

As I mentioned earlier in the book, it is a great idea to stare at yourself in the mirror and study the various aspects of your face. Most people believe they have a fairly good understanding of self. However, there are always characteristics of the face that can unlock a deeper understanding of why a person reacts in a predictable pattern. For example, most people are unaware when they are defensive. They react to certain triggers, but they are often unaware of their reactions. When you pay attention to your emotional triggers and study your own face, you can begin tracing back through your history to discover when you have told yourself a story that does not serve you in your pursuit of success.

Pay particular attention to your nose bridge and look for defensiveness bumps. Next, pay attention to any notches on your ears (if you are past 18 years of age) and recall what might have happened at a given point in your history that changed your perception. Finally, pay attention to any bags under your eyes. These either indicate a medical condition (deficiency in certain vitamins), or they indicate unresolved emotional issues. If you have a bag under your right eye, a notch on your right ear at the 20 year-old mark, and a bump on your nose at the 20-year old level, something happened when you were 20 that you have not dealt with. You need to work through your past in order to live more fully in the present. Study yourself and understand your tendencies for every aspect of what the face can tell you. Understand the story of you, and you will position yourself for success in all that you do.

Ministry

I have a number of friends and several family members who are in ministry. When they are counseling people, praying for people, or just connecting with people, the more they can know about them, the easier it is for people to open up and really deal with what is going on in their lives. When you meet someone new at a ministry event, you will already know what some of their struggles are. For example, if a person has ear lobes that seem to angle out from their head and their gum line shows when they smile, they tend to take on other people's problems and feel responsible for calming people down. They tend to give more than they expect to get in relationships, and it eventually burns them out and causes them a good deal of stress. When you understand them, you can comfort them and let them know that they don't have to take on the problems of the world. They simply need to live into their purpose and let other people own their own problems. You can tell them that it is okay for them to take a break from others and have quiet time to pray and meditate and build themselves back up.

By knowing things about others before the conversation even starts, you are prepared to connect with them and build credibility with them. People are absolutely fascinated when you know things about them that they think others shouldn't be able to know. They are pulled toward trust when you encourage them with things that are actually relevant to their lives. So often, people just want to know that someone else cares for them. They want to know God's assurance and know He is there. Understanding of people in ministry is a very delicate and personal way of connecting with people. It should never be used as a "show," but should be used to help, heal, and empower people to become the best version of themselves possible.

Fundraising

Raising money requires more than just a good pitch. It requires connecting with the right people and building an emotional desire in them. To give yourself an advantage in the process, you can create a profile of the donors who are a great fit. Keep in mind that different profiles of people will give to different causes. Just because your cause is amazing in your own mind doesn't mean that others will see the same things that you see. You have to find a way to appeal to that specific person or a specific group/type of people.

One on one asks are the ideal way to use face reading. When asking for a large donation one-on-one, you will need to prepare for it in the same way you prepare for selling a product or service. You need to know how they evaluate themselves (chin). You need to know how they make decisions (forehead). You need to know how much time to spend building rapport (eyebrows). You need to know how to structure you messaging (ears). With fundraising, you also need to know how mission driven the person is (septum of the nose). By knowing these things, you can adapt your presentation to meet the processing requirements of that person. You learn to get away from a one size fits all model. As you move toward this advanced adaptation to the individual, the person being asked will feel more like the offer was tailor-made for them. They will be more engaged in the conversation. And, they will be much more likely to say YES to what you are offering. People give because the offer seems to be an extension of who they see themselves as. They feel a connection and a desire to contribute. They don't give out of obligation like they did in previous generations. This is important for you to remember because your success in fundraising is dependent on you fully grasping who you are asking for money and how they measure their purpose in the process.

Finally, when you build a profile of the ideal giver, you are looking for the common characteristics of your top 20 donors. Study the faces of the people who give the most and then use social media to find people who have the highest likelihood of contributing to your cause. Be genuine and seek out the right people. This is best for them as well as best for you and your organization.

11 QUICK REFERENCE GUIDE

Reading People At A Glance – Quick Reference Guide

When you are working with individuals and need to get a quick read for who they are and what the best methodology for communicating with them would be, using face reading is extremely effective. This is the science of facial structure as it relates to beliefs and thoughts. The face itself is a reflection of the thoughts and belief patterns of a person. At a glance, you can tell if a person is logical or emotion, relational or task oriented, and lots more. For the purposes of getting a quick read of a person, there are five (5) main areas that should be focused on related to the face.

Forehead – The forehead will be either flat across or rounded. This area of the face will indicate what the person needs in the way of information focus in order to process efficiently. For example, the flat across forehead (less rounded) requires facts, data, and logic. They need to hear the justification and need it backed up by what can be proven in order to believe you. In healthcare, this is the person who will want to see the chart or see the test results in order to buy in the what you are prescribing. The person with the rounded forehead needs emotional appeal in order to trust you. They are not looking for as much of the data as they are the connection. Typically, this person will require an additional 1 to 2 minutes of rapport building before they will be cooperative as a family member or patient. If you can keep in mind the best cognitive appeal (facts versus emotions) when engaging with a person initially, this will position you to gain their trust and their cooperation.

Eyebrows – The eyebrows will be in one of two primary shapes with the possibility of an arch or no arch in the eyebrows. The two primary shapes are rounded and flat. With each of these, there is the possibility of a spike on either or both sides of the brow. The flat eyebrows indicate a rational approach to people. This rational or logical approach to people means that the person will tend to engage for reasons that they can easily justify. In other words, they will have to see the benefit for themselves and the other person in order to enter into a relationship with them. The rounded eyebrows indicate a relational and emotional approach to people. These are the people that generally find it easier to engage with others. On the left hand side of the face, people will represent their beliefs about their personal lives. On the right-hand side of the face, people will represent their beliefs about their professional lives. It is possible to have a slightly different shape, as well as differed positioning of the eyebrows from one side of the face to the other. When a person has a spike in their left eyebrow (a place in the eyebrow hair that goes up from the rest of the brow in a spike or sharp arc), this indicates a need for control in their personal lives. It does not mean that they have control, just that they have a need for it. When a person has a spike in their right eyebrow, this indicates a need for control in their professional lives. If they have a spike on both sides, they just need control. ☺ The positioning of the eyebrow has meaning as well. The primary thing to look for is whether or not the eyebrow comes down just below the brow ridge. If it does, this indicates quick input-output. This is the person that often will say what is in their mind, even if they shouldn't. They have a weaker filter between their brain and mouth.

Nose – There are two primary aspects of the nose to pay attention to. The first aspect is whether or not the person has a bump/ridge on their nose. The bridge of the nose will rise up, which represents the bump. This is the defensiveness bump. When a person has this on their nose, it indicates that they will "come out swinging" if they get backed into a corner. They are often very nice until they reach the point of being pushed too far. The second aspect of the nose is the lines on the sides of the nostrils. You could trace your finger from the lower corners of the nose (beside the face) up and around the sides of the nose toward the tip of the nose. The deeper those lines are, the more fiercely independent the person is. When a person is fiercely independent, they need choices, not instructions. For example, you would let them know that you needed their help to achieve a certain outcome and then ask them what the best process would be to get there. Another option would be to ask them whether they would rather choice A, choice B, or choice C and then let them decide which is best for them.

Chin – Just above the end of the chin, between the chin and the lower lip, will either be the presence of a line in an arch/half-moon or the presence of smooth skin. When the line is present, this is known as the "verbal affirmation" line. It indicates that this person has a stronger need for appreciation when they do a good job or when they go above and beyond what is required. It is ideal to let them know what you appreciate about their specific behavior and how it has helped you. When this person does not get the appreciation that they crave/need, they will often let other people know that they are feeling undervalued. The second aspect of the chin that is relevant is the shape of the chin itself. It can be squared off / flat on the bottom, which indicates a strong focus on goals and achievement with a low tolerance for whining and complaining. If this is the case, this person will be driven by and focused on achieving specific goals. They often come to work each day with a plan or a task list that they want and need to accomplish. The chin can be rounded, which indicates a focus on connection with people and the development of relationships. If this is the case, the person will approach work from the perspective of how they relate to others and what their relationships are like with others. Finally, the chin can come to a point. This is often a driven person, but they have become disillusioned with relationships. They are frustrated with being let down by others and don't feel that they can count on other people to do what they are supposed to do. Because of this, they are more prone to lashing out at others and making rash and aggressive responses to not having their needs met.

Ears – The final area to quickly read a person is their ears. The ears will be small and back towards the head, slightly larger and often sticking out more from the head, or will have a larger inner ear ridge than the outer ear cup. These three ear structures represent the learning and language patterns of the person. The ears that are smaller and closer to the head are the visual communicators and thinkers. They need visual words such as "picture this" and "I can see what you mean," or they need the use of comparisons in order to fully grasp a concept. You could say, "Doing this will be just like when we did that (description of another time). The larger ears that are often out away from the head represents the auditory thinker and learner. These types can hear and remember things very well. They often did well in public school because of the auditory nature of lectures. They will use words like "think, process, dialogue, and listen." The final type of processor/learner is represented by an ear that has a larger inner ear ridge than the outer one. This is the kinesthetic processor/learner. This person process information through action and intuition. Very often, you will see that nurses in a hospital setting are kinesthetic in their thoughts, while doctors are one of the other types, often auditory. This can pose a challenge, in that the doctors give instruction in their language pattern while the nurses need the instruction in their own. The kinesthetic thinker will use words like, "feel, my gut tells me, move, and act." If a person can tweak the words that they use, in order to stimulate the thoughts of the other person, the other person will be much better off and more able to understand the speaker.

Keep in mind that the quality of your communication is measured solely by the quality of the response that you get from others. If you are not getting a good response, you are responsible for changing your approach to that person or those people. I would encourage you to read this several times in order to get a full grasp of these five facial components. Consider the components in conjunction with one another in order to get the best read on another person.

12 ADDITIONAL RESOURCES

A Video of me reading the faces of the Montoya Twinz and their family: http://bit.ly/montoyatwins

A Video of me reading the faces of the Student Leadership Team at West Texas A & M University: http://bit.ly/wtleaders

Find Additional Training On Face Reading:
www.facereadingbook.com
www.jodyholland.com
Bit.ly/jodytubesub

Direct Links To Jody's Books

Title	Bit Link
6 Demons of Fear	http://bit.ly/6demonsbook
Hypnotic Selling	http://bit.ly/hypnoticbook
Leadership Evo	http://bit.ly/leadershipevo
Success: A 12 Step Program	http://bit.ly/success12step
25 Activities In A Bag	http://bit.ly/25activities
Yay! I'm A Supervisor	http://bit.ly/yaysupervisorbook
Selling With Honor	http://bit.ly/sellinghonor
Turn Me On	http://bit.ly/turnmeonbook
A Life of Miracles: The First 60 Lessons	http://bit.ly/alifeofmiracles1
Just Make Time	http://bit.ly/justmaketime
The Quest	http://bit.ly/thequestbook
My Judo Life	http://bit.ly/myjudolife
Living The Quest	http://bit.ly/livingthequest
Breakthrough Leadership	http://bit.ly/breakthroughleader
Psyche of Success: Volume 1	http://bit.ly/psycheofsuccess1

ABOUT THE AUTHOR

Jody Holland has a B.A. in Communications and a M.S. in Psychology. He has received specialized training and certifications in team-building, leadership, management, face reading and personnel testing. A strong advocate for helping people discover and utilize their strengths to the fullest, Jody has founded several companies with a focus on enhancing leadership effectiveness. Jody has had the opportunity to train and do business in 14 countries and all across the United States. Jody has worked with the Fortune 50 as well as small businesses from all industries. He has been contracted by both universities and junior colleges to teach continuing education courses on leadership, sales, and management. Jody has been the keynote speaker more than **300** times at conferences and has trained more than **200,000** leaders. He has been the executive coach for **20+** CEO's and more than **100** top executives. He has helped increased net profits by more than $50 million across his client base.

Jody is the author of 17 books, which can be found at bit.ly/jodyholland, including books on face reading, leadership, time management, sales, personal development, and organizational development. Jody has co-authored more than 30 training programs on supervision, management, and leadership. He has authored courses on face reading, sales, service, leadership and management.

Jody started his business in 1999 and is still growing and expanding his reach today. Check him out at www.JodyHolland.com.

Made in the USA
Middletown, DE
06 February 2022